MEDICAID
101

The Ultimate Guide to NJ Medicaid Services, Planning and Secrets

Charles C. Bratton II, Esq., LLM

Table of Contents

CHAPTER 1

WHAT IS MEDICAID?

If you were to ask middle or high school students, I'd be willing to bet that a good number of them would tell you that they do, in fact, enjoy learning. What they don't enjoy is how the information they're learning is presented to them. Everybody has a way of learning that they enjoy the best so that they glean the most knowledge from what's being presented.

Even in our adult lives, I'd be willing to say with relative certainty that there are just some things that, while we know they may be important, we just don't enjoy hearing about. Take politics, for example. Yes, it is important to know what our candidates and leaders stand for so we know whom it is we should support. Most times, though, it can seem like a jumbled, confusing mess that we feel much better off just leaving alone.

In the same way as they do politics, some people simply choose to believe their doctor when it comes to government programs like Medicaid or Medicare, simply because there is so much information to learn and remember about each—never mind the fact the rules are constantly changing—that it can seem as though we're drowning in them.

It is with this thought in mind that we approach the topic now. We get it. Some of us just *don't* get it; some of us need to have this information given to us in bite-sized form so that it's more easily mentally digestible. If you're reading this and thinking to yourself, "Hey, that's me!" then you're in luck. It is our goal to present to you some information about Medicaid in a way that's not only easy to understand, but hopefully entertaining to read. We also know that if something is entertaining, people are more likely to stick with it to the end, which is what we want.

By the end of this, we want you to come away feeling as though you not only learned a thing or two, but were also able to understand it without having to consult a dictionary or some book full of legal jargon. With that as our goal, let's get started.

*****

MEDICAID VS. MEDICARE

As with anything we don't understand, if we're going to be talking about something as big and complex as Medicaid, it would be greatly beneficial to us to figure out exactly what it is before we go any further. Many of us may have heard about it (and Medicare) all our lives, but may not have a good grasp on what all it entails.

So, let's change that now.

As we begin this journey together, it is important that we talk not only about Medicaid, but also Medicare too, so let's make that our starting point now.

MEDICARE—WHAT IS IT?

Simply put, Medicare is a government program that gives health care coverage (that is, health insurance) to those people who are 65 or older, those who are under 65 but who get Social Security Disability Insurance (SSDI) for a predetermined amount of time, or who are under 65 but have End-Stage Renal Disease (ESRD). The program is run by the Centers for Medicare & Medicaid Services, or CMS, and is partially funded by the Social Security and Medicare taxes that you pay on your income, partially by premiums that those who have Medicare pay, and partially through the federal budget.

Once you have become eligible to receive Medicare, you can then take part in Original Medicare, which is the more traditional fee-for-service program offered by the government directly, or you may choose the Medicare Advantage Plan—a private insurance plan offered by those companies that have a contract with Medicare (that is, with the federal government).

It is very important that we understand the coverage choices we have when it comes to Medicare and to choose our type of coverage very carefully. After all, we want to have the coverage that is going to be the best for us in the long run. To put it another way, how we choose to get our benefits and who we receive those benefits from can affect how much we have to pay out-of-pocket and where we can go to get the care that we need. As an example, Original Medicare provides us coverage to go to almost any and all doctors and hospitals in the nation. Conversely, Medicare Advantage Plans come with some restrictions, which means that we'd have much more limited access to doctors and hospitals. Even so, Medicare Advantage Plans do have some benefits that Original Medicare does not—such as routine vision or dental care.

Keep in mind that you *do* still have Medicare if you take part in the Medicare Advantage Plan. That means you'll still have to pay a monthly Part B premium (and the Part A premium, if you have it. We'll cover each part more in depth here in a little bit.) For now, just know that every Medicare Advantage Plan has to give individuals the same Part A and Part B services given by Original Medicare, but it is able to do so while having different rules, costs, and restrictions that could potentially affect both how and when you receive care.

Also, it is important to remember that if you get health coverage from your union or either your current or former employer when you become eligible to receive Medicare, you might be automatically enrolled in a Medicare Advantage Plan they happen to sponsor. If that sounds a little unfair to you, fear not. You do have some choices in the matter. You could, for instance, stay with this particular plan, switch to Original Medicare, or enroll in a completely different Medicare Advantage Plan altogether. No matter which option you choose, though, you'll want to speak to your employer or union before making any decisions regarding this.

We'll get more into the differences between the two programs a little later on in the chapter, but for now, just remember that Medicare and Medicaid are, in fact, different from each other. Medicaid, as you're likely aware, is yet another government-run program that gives health insurance to individuals. It is also funded by the federal government as well and is run in partnership between the government and the states to help cover those people who have a limited income. While it does, indeed, vary by state, Medicaid might be a valid option for those people who fall below a certain level of income who also meet certain other criteria (such as age, disability status, pregnancy, etc.), or it could be available to everyone who falls below a certain income level. An important distinction to make between Medicare and Medicaid is that, unlike Medicaid, one's eligibility for Medicare does not hinge on their income or assets.

Those who have Medicare get a red-white-and-blue Original Medicare card. If you decide to receive coverage through Original Medicare, you'll need to show this card whenever you receive any services. If you decide to go the route of the Medicare Advantage Plan, you'll still receive an Original Medicare card, but will need to show your private plan card when receiving services instead.

Most important of all: No matter how you receive your health care benefits from Medicare, never give your Medicare number to anyone other than your doctors or any other health care providers!

*****

Now that we know what Medicare *is*, let's take some time to look at what it is it actually covers.

To start out, there are, in fact, four different parts of Medicare. Each of those four parts will cover different services. The four parts of Medicare are: Part A, Part B, Part C, and Part D.

If you have Original Medicare, that is run by the federal government directly. It is also the way that a majority of people receive their Medicare benefits, and is made up of two parts—Parts A and B. Let's take a closer look at each now:

1. **Part A (Hospital Insurance):** This covers a majority of medically necessary hospital care, skilled nursing facility, home health, and hospice care. It is, in fact, free if you have both worked and paid Social Security taxes for at least 40 calendar quarters (that is, 10 years). If you have worked and paid taxes for less than that amount of time, you will have to pay a monthly premium.

2. **Part B (Medical Insurance):** Part B will cover a majority of medically necessary doctors' visits, preventative care, durable medical equipment, any hospital outpatient services, lab tests, x-rays, mental health care, and a few home health and ambulance services. You'll have a monthly premium for this coverage.

*****

Medicare Part D is known as outpatient Prescription Drug Insurance, and it does exactly what it says. Unlike the other two, however, Part D is only available via private insurance companies that have contracts with the government, but it is never directly provided by the government itself. If you want Part D services, you're going to have to choose the Part D coverage that will work with your

Medicare health benefits.

If you've got Original Medicare, you're going to need to pick a stand-alone Part D plan (or PDP).

Perhaps most different of all, Medicare Part C is not a separate benefit. Instead, it is the part of Medicare policy that gives private health insurance companies the right to provide those in their care with Medicare benefits. These plans—like HMOs and PPOs—are what's known as those Medicare Advantage Plans we've been talking about. If you so choose, you can receive your Medicare coverage through just such a plan instead of opting for Original Medicare.

Medicare Advantage Plans have to, at the very least, give individuals the same benefits as Original Medicare (those who are covered under Parts A and B), but as we mentioned earlier, it can do so with different rules, costs and restrictions to coverage. Most of the time, you'll get Part D as a part of your benefits package that comes with your Medicare Advantage Plan. Several different plans are available aside from the two that we listed above, and you could potentially pay a monthly premium for this coverage along with the premium you're paying for Part B as well.

*****

MEDICAID

We've covered Medicare pretty well for now, so let's switch gears and spend some time taking a look at Medicaid. Technically, it *is* the point of the entire book, so it would be good to do that! With that said, this section is going to cover Medicaid in New Jersey specifically. To find out the type of Medicaid and Medicaid-related programs are available in your state, as well as what they cover, and who might be eligible, you should contact a local office of your state's own Medicaid program. In order to find that Medicaid office, check out the federal government's Benefits.gov website and choose your own state.

Doing so will take you to a page that has contact information for your state's Medicaid program and information about its local offices.

MEDICAID IN NEW JERSEY

As it is in other states across the nation, the Medicaid program in New Jersey is designed to give medical help to those people and families who have low incomes to be able to get the medical care that they need. In New Jersey alone, almost 1.8 million people are covered by Medicaid. What's more—enrollment in the program has increased by 37% in the four years between 2013 and 2016. That's a pretty impressive jump!

Now, I know what you might be thinking. "That's great and all, but what exactly does Medicaid actually have to do with the government?"

Right?

That's certainly a fair question, and I'm glad you asked.

The United States government launched the Medicaid program all the way back in 1965, and the program is currently run on a state-by-state basis, meaning rules and regulations can vary depending on where you are in the country.

As we just said, Medicaid coverage can and does vary by state, but all Medicaid programs are run at a state-level by that state's health department. And while each state's program must comply with federal regulations that have been set by the government, the program itself isn't actually controlled *by* the government.

Of course, there's going to be some things that stay the same in every place with regard to information. As an example, in New Jersey, Medicaid will cover some services that aren't covered in other states. Conversely, other states may cover things that aren't covered in New Jersey. Price is another area that can fluctuate between states as well.

Certain insurance holders won't pay a dime due to low income, while still others might pay something in the form of a monthly premium or a medical co-pay.

Up to now, we've talked a lot about services and all that Medicaid provides, but how exactly do we find out whether or not we qualify to receive it?

As we've said, Medicaid was put in place to help those low-income families or individuals to get the help they need. Determining whether or not one is eligible to receive Medicaid benefits in New Jersey is more dependent on the income level of the person or persons who are applying. Only those who are within the right range will be able to receive help and benefits from Medicaid. Along with income level, there are other eligibility requirements that relate to state residency, legal status within the country and a host of other things we won't get into right now. No matter what, however, applicants in New Jersey have to meet all the eligibility requirements if they want to qualify for the program.

If you find that you are indeed eligible for Medicaid assistance, you can begin the application process whenever you'd like. There are a number of ways available to you to apply, and we'll get into those a little bit later on in the book. The good thing to remember now, though, is that those qualified individuals and families are able to choose whatever type of application that is best able to meet their specific needs.

*****

QUALIFICATIONS FOR MEDICAID IN NEW JERSEY

Thanks to an election to expand Medicaid, eligibility benefits now cover thousands of patients who need them. Now that there has been an increase in applications, the qualifications or requirements have also changed.

Those who are aged, blind or otherwise disabled can now get top-quality care. However, in order to truly understand who meets these requirements (and thus, who is eligible), you've got to know the specifics.

Fear not.

We'll get to that more in-depth in the next chapter.

For now, let's continue on here and finish up this one by discussing the cost and coverage of Medicaid in New Jersey.

*****

COST AND COVERAGE OF MEDICAID IN NEW JERSEY

The truth is that the costs, coverage and even the types of Medicaid insurance in New Jersey are different from those medical assistance programs that are found in other states. New Jersey Medicaid is also known as NJ FamilyCare, and it gives health care to those qualified individuals—like children, pregnant women, the aged, blind, disabled, childless couples, single adults, as well as parents or caretaker relatives.

The services that New Jersey Medicaid offer are given to people using a detailed health program initiative. To finish up this chapter, we'll spend some time taking a look at four areas. They are:

- **How much does Medicaid cost in New Jersey?**

- **What services are covered in New Jersey?**

- **What does Medicaid *not* cover in New Jersey?**

- **The types of Medicaid insurance available in New Jersey**

*****

We've got a few things to get through, so let's start at the best place—the beginning.

HOW MUCH DOES MEDICAID COST IN NEW JERSEY?

How much Medicaid will cost can be estimated based on the beneficiary. Some types of medical services are fully covered, but some must still be paid for—though at a low cost. It should be said, though, that some individuals with Medicaid coverage are exempt from making any type of payments. Those include those children under the age of 19 and pregnant women.

Once your application for services has been approved, you will then be contacted via mail with information pertaining to your New Jersey Medicaid coverage premium. The cost estimates for that premium will be dependent on numerous things, like family income size, number of people covered, and so forth.

First payments should be sent as soon as the monthly premium is known. For those new members, the benefits will go into effect only after a full payment has been received. After you enroll in Medicaid coverage, members are then billed by the month. If you happen to be a patient who qualifies to receive full Medicaid benefits, you may get statements from time to time, depending on the services and supplies you need or use, even though you might not get a monthly bill. The aged receiving Medicaid will not pay a premium other than their portion of the cost share via their income but we'll get into that a little later.

*****

SERVICES COVERED IN NEW JERSEY

Now that we've seen the cost estimates for Medicaid, we've got to then understand what exactly Medicaid will cover. The following services are covered for eligible members:

- Transportation to get medical services or items covered by Medicaid.

- Durable medical equipment and supplies, X-rays and laboratory services.

- Clinical services, like physical, occupational and speech therapies.

- Both inpatient and outpatient hospital care, hospice care and rehabilitation services, like audiology.

- Any orthopedic shoes, braces, artificial limbs, hearing aids or eyeglasses.

- Services from professionals like optometrists, psychologists, podiatrists, dentists and chiropractors.

- Personal care assistants, medical day care, nursing home care and home health care services.

- Prescription drugs via a pharmacy (including a few OTC medications)

- Any and all medical services provided via physician in a clinic, office, or another medical facility.

- Any mental health services given in a hospital outpatient department, approved mental health clinic or a doctor's office.

*****

SERVICES NOT COVERED

Even though there are a great number of services that are covered by Medicaid, there are still some that are not. For some of those services, preauthorization is required to handle something on your behalf. For others, you're going to need to pay out-of-pocket costs.

Most generally, New Jersey Medicaid doesn't cover the services that fall under these guidelines or categories:

- **The provider hasn't received a program payment from either your NJ Medicaid Health Plan or Medicaid FFS.**

- **The added protections do not apply under New Jersey state and federal law.**

- **The service that is offered isn't considered a trauma or emergency as defined by New Jersey state law.**

- **Your medical provider doesn't normally participate in New Jersey Medicaid Health Plans or does not as it relates to that specific service.**

- **The service is deemed medically unnecessary.**

- **The service is given out-of-state without prior authorization.**

*****

Making use of the aforementioned guidelines will help you to better determine what is or isn't covered by Medicaid in New Jersey. For those services *not* covered, the provider is required to inform you in writing about his or her decision. Also, you must voluntarily agree to pay either part of or the entire amount of the provider's charges for services before they are given.

Eligibility for Medicaid coverage when it comes to any medical services is dependent on the benefits package you have been approved for. Medicaid services in New Jersey are offered in five benefits packages.

They are:

1. **Medicaid and New Jersey FamilyCare A**

2. **DDD Clients**

3. **New Jersey FamilyCare B and C**

4. **New Jersey FamilyCare D**

5. **New Jersey FamilyCare ABP**

While a majority of services are, in fact, covered in full, there are a few that are given only on a fee-for-service basis. As an example, an abortion or any related services are not covered on any benefits. The only exception to this is if the abortion must be done to save the mother's life.

Still, other types of NJ Medicaid services may be fully covered or come with some restrictions across a few benefits packages. Another example: All packages cover acupuncture services except for NJ FamilyCare D—which only covers it when it is performed as an anesthetic for surgeries.

You should work to confirm what Medicaid does not cover with your health plan provider before getting a treatment or procedure. Any services given that are not covered by Medicaid might need to be fully paid for out-of-pocket or via a third-party insurance company.

It is also important to note that a lot of medical providers and doctor's offices are willing to work with payment plans. If you plan on getting a service that isn't covered by Medicaid, be sure and ask them about any payment plan options they have available. That way, you can go ahead and get the treatment or procedure you need and then break those payments into smaller amounts over a set period of time instead of worrying about trying to get everything taken care of all at once. When you're facing a procedure of any kind, you have enough to worry about, and having to figure out payment shouldn't be one of them.

TYPES OF MEDICAID INSURANCE IN NEW JERSEY

The types of Medicaid insurance plans in New Jersey may differ from those available in other states. When you go to apply for Medicaid coverage, you'll need to pick a health plan to cover medical services. Each and every county in New Jersey has at least three different plans that you can choose from. Plans available include the following:

- **Aetna Better Health of New Jersey**

- **AMERIGROUP New Jersey, Inc.**

- **Horizon NJ Health**

- **United Healthcare Community Plan**

- **WellCare**

There are also a variety of Medicaid types of insurance that cater to those patients in different age groups with or without certain medical conditions. The insurances will have different guidelines and limits on coverage, but in many cases, a service will also be covered by Medicaid when your health insurance pays for a service that Medicaid covers—that is, so long as it doesn't go over your allocated reimbursement rate.

Every type of Medicaid insurance needs to be renewed every year. During this process, both the financial and family situation of the applicant(s) will be evaluated to look for any changes. Failing to renew this insurance could result in interruptions in or loss of coverage altogether.

*****

QUICK REVIEW

Before moving onto the next chapter, let's quickly look at a review of the differences between Medicaid and Medicare.

As we stated previously, each is different from the other, but both are programs run by the government. They were created in 1965 as a way for older or lower-income Americans to get health insurance when they were unable to afford private health insurance. Both programs were a part of President Lyndon Johnson's "Great Society" vision of a social commitment to meeting the health care needs of individuals. Both Medicaid and Medicare are social insurance programs that let the financial hardships that come with illness to be shared by both healthy and sick persons alike, as well as those well-off and low-income families too.

Again, the differences are as follows:

- **Medicare:** A federal program that gives coverage to those who are aged 65+ or who have a severe disability, regardless of their level of income.

- **Medicaid:** Both a state and federal program that gives coverage to those who have a very low income and assets.

- If you find yourself eligible for both Medicare and Medicaid (known as dual eligibility), you may have both. Medicare and Medicaid will then work in tandem to give you a great amount of health coverage.

- **Also, be aware that Medicare WILL NOT pay for ongoing long-term care**, so that is a good reason to consider Medicaid as well.

*****

That about wraps it up for this initial chapter. We've already covered a lot, but there's still a lot more to go. I hope that it's been an enjoyable and informative read for you so far.

In the next chapter, we'll look more at the general eligibility requirements to receive Medicaid.

Let's go!

CHAPTER 2

GENERAL ELIGIBILITY REQUIREMENTS

Welcome back!

We just got done talking about what exactly Medicaid is, and now we'll spend this chapter discussing the eligibility requirements for Medicaid. As we did before, we'll talk more about the general requirements, and then move onto New Jersey specifically. We will also look at the requirements for both single and married applicants and see how they differ. Finally, we'll end the chapter by defining the look back period—what it is and how it affects us—and what exactly a QIT (or Qualified Income Trust) is.

We've got a lot to get through, and I'm glad you came back, so sit back, relax and let's talk.

*****

ELIGIBILITY

Before we get into the meat of this chapter, let's spend a few minutes briefly in an overview. So, we already know that Medicaid is a program designed by the federal government and carried out both on

16

the federal as well as state level. Together with the Children's Health Insurance Program (or CHIP), Medicaid gives health coverage to over 72.5 Americans—including children, pregnant women, parents, seniors, and those people with disabilities. It is, in fact, the number one largest source of health coverage in the United States. That's interesting and also quite impressive!

In order to be able to participate in the Medicaid program, federal law mandates that individual states have to provide coverage for certain groups of individuals. These mandatory eligibility groups include the following: low-income families, pregnant women and children, and those people who are getting Supplemental Security Income (or SSI). The states also have more options in regard to coverage and might choose to cover some other groups as well. Such groups might be those who are getting home and community-based services as well as those children in foster care who aren't eligible any other way.

Thanks to the Affordable Care Act of 2010, each state had the opportunity to widen the reach of Medicaid in order to cover almost every low-income American under the age of 65. With regard to children, this helped extend eligibility to at least 133 percent of the federal poverty level (FPL) in each state. What's good about this is that most states will cover those children to higher income levels), and those states were also given the chance to extend eligibility to adults as well, to those whose income sat at or below 133 percent of the FPL. Most of the states have opted to expand coverage to adults, and those that haven't yet can choose to do that any time they like.

DETERMINING ELIGIBILITY FOR MEDICAID

Financial Eligibility

The Affordable Care Act that we just talked about above created a new way to figure out income eligibility (that is, financial eligibility) for Medicaid. This new method is based off of what's known as

Modified Adjusted Gross Income (or MAGI). This method is used to figure out financial eligibility for not only Medicaid, but CHIP and premium tax credits and cost sharing reductions that are available through the health insurance marketplace too. In using only one set of rules for counting income and a single application across programs, the Affordable Care Act greatly simplified how people can apply and enroll in the right program that meets their specific needs.

In fact, MAGI is the foundation for figuring out the financial eligibility for Medicaid for a majority of children, pregnant women, parents and adults. This method looks at any taxable income and tax filing relationships in order to figure out if someone is financially eligible to receive Medicaid. MAGI also took the place of the previously used process for calculating eligibility for Medicaid, which was based on the methods used by another program, the Aid to Families with Dependent Children (or AFDC), which ended in 1996. The MAGI method simply doesn't allow for any disregards in income that vary according to state or eligibility group, and it doesn't allow for an asset or resource test either.

It is possible, though, that some people could be exempt from income rules based on MAGI, however. These could include those whose eligibility is based on something like blindness, disability or age (65 years or older). Determining Medicaid eligibility for these individuals is most often done via the income methods of the supplemental security income (SSI) program that is given by the Social Security Administration. It should be said that some states, known as 209(b) states, sometimes use certain criteria that are more restrictive than SSI's but will normally still apply SSI methodologies. Determining a person's eligibility for the Medicare Savings Program—that Medicaid uses to pay Medicare premiums, deductibles and/or any coinsurance costs for those beneficiaries who are eligible for both programs (referred to normally as dual eligibles)—is also done with SSI methods as well.

It should be said that there are some Medicaid eligibility groups that don't need a determination of income via the Medicaid agency. This coverage could be based on enrollment in some other program, like SSI or the breast and cervical cancer treatment and prevention program. For those children who have an adoption assistance agreement in effect, under title IV-E of the Social Security Act, they are automatically eligible for Medicaid. For young adults, if they meet the requirements of eligibility as a former recipient of foster care, they are eligible regardless of their level of income.

Non-Financial Eligibility

In order to be eligible to receive Medicaid, one must not only meet financial requirements, but nonfinancial ones as well. Those Medicaid beneficiaries must normally be residents of the state in which they are applying for or receiving Medicaid. They have to either be residents of the United States or certain qualified non-citizens, like lawful permanent residents. Also, some eligibility groups are limited by age, or by pregnancy or parenting status as well.

Effective Date of Coverage

Once someone has been determined as eligible to receive Medicaid, their coverage goes into effect on the date of application or the first day of the month of application. Benefits could also be covered retroactively for a period of up to 3 months before the month of application, but only if the person would have eligible if he or she had applied during that period. Often times, coverage stops at the end of the month in which an individual no longer meets the requirements necessary to receive eligibility for Medicaid.

Medically Needy

The states also have the option to create a "medically needy program" for those people who suffer from significant health issues, but whose income is too high to qualify for Medicaid otherwise under the other eligibility groups. Those deemed as medically needy still have the opportunity to become eligible by "spending down" that amount of income that is above a particular state's standard of medically needy income. Spending down happens when someone acquires expenses for both medical and remedial care for which they don't have any health insurance. Once those expenses go beyond the difference between the person's income and the state's medically needy income level (otherwise known as the "spend down amount"), he or she can then be eligible to receive Medicaid. Medicaid will then pay the cost of those services that go beyond what the person needed to incur with regard to expenses in order that they might become eligible.

Aside from those states that have a medically needy program, those 209(b) states we mentioned before have to also allow spend down to those income eligibility levels eligibility groups based on things like blindness, disability, or age (65 and up), even if the state has a medically needy program too. There are a total of thirty-six states plus the District of Columbia that make use of spend-down programs, either in the form of medically needy programs or as 209(b) states.

Before we take a look at eligibility requirements for individuals and couples, let's take a quick detour to see some topics related to this discussion as well.

RELATED TOPICS

Spousal Impoverishment: This protects the spouse of a Medicaid applicant or beneficiary who needs to have coverage for long-term services and supports (or LTSS), in an institution or home, or some other community-based setting, from becoming impoverished just to provide the spouse in need of LTSS the ability to get Medicaid coverage for those services.

Treatment of Trusts: When either an individual, the person's spouse, or anyone who is acting on behalf of the individual creates a trust using some of the individual's funds, said trust can then be considered as available to the individual for the purpose of determining their eligibility to receive Medicaid, depending on the type of trust, the assets with which it is funded, and its purpose.

Transfer of Assets for Less Than Fair Market Value: Those Medicaid beneficiaries that need LTSS can (and will) be denied LTSS coverage if they have transferred any assets for less than their fair market value during that five-year period that came before their application for Medicaid. This applies when assets are either transferred, sold, or gifted for any less than they are actually worth by either individuals or their spouses who need LTSS in a long-term care facility or who wish to get home and community-based waiver services.

Estate Recovery: The state Medicaid programs have to recover from a Medicaid enrollee's estate the cost of some benefits that have been paid on the enrollee's behalf. These include things like nursing facility services, home and community-based services, and related hospital and prescription drug services too. State Medicaid programs can also recover for other Medicaid benefits as well, except for Medicare cost-sharing benefits that are paid on behalf of the beneficiaries of the Medicare Savings Program.

Third Party Liability: This refers to those third parties who have a legal obligation to pay for some or all of the cost of any medical services that are given to a Medicaid beneficiary. Some examples of this include Medicare or some other health insurance a person may have that will cover a portion of the cost of medical service. If a third party has an obligation like that, then Medicaid will only pay for that particular portion of it.

Waivers and Demonstrations: States have the ability to apply to the Centers for Medicare and Medicaid Services for waivers in order to give Medicaid to those populations beyond what can traditionally be covered under the state's own plan. However, some states may have more state only programs in order to give medical help to certain low-income people who don't otherwise qualify to receive Medicaid. No federal funds are given to state only programs, however, so it's something to keep in mind.

*****

Now that we've got a general overview of eligibility, let's pull in a little bit to better focus on requirements for both single and married applicants. As we did before, we'll be looking at New Jersey specifically, so things could be slightly different in your state, and it would be beneficial to look up some things pertaining to wherever you are.

PLANNING FOR MEDICAID IN NEW JERSEY

The old saying of "Time waits for no one," is especially true. Time marches on whether we want it to or not, and people are getting older all the time. That age is really having an effect on not only people's health but their money as well. That's why it can be (and is) so important to have a plan of what you're going to do when the time comes to pay for things like assisted living, nursing homes or long-term care.

If you're both medically and financially able to do so, you should look into getting long-term care insurance. If you cannot, or don't qualify due to a medical condition or if the premiums don't allow it, you should definitely consider asset protection planning now in order to qualify for Medicaid benefits in the event of a crisis.

Like we said before, in order to qualify for those Medicaid benefits, a person must first meet the eligibility requirements. These requirements include meeting both medical and financial standards. We'll touch on some things we've covered above, but go into a bit more depth this time as well.

22

Let's go.

FINANCIAL ELIGIBILITY

If an applicant is single, he or she can have up to and no mo_ $2,000 of countable resources in New Jersey. If the applicant is married and both husband and wife apply together, those countable resources may not exceed $3,000.

So, what do we mean when we say "countable resources?"

Keep reading and let's find out together.

COUNTABLE RESOURCES VS. EXEMPT RESOURCES

There are certain resources (or assets) that the individual or family has that Medicaid considers to be exempt. These resources, then, are not counted when assessing a person's financial eligibility to receive Medicaid. These exempt resources are different from countable (or non-exempt) resources. Generally, the resources that follow are those primarily exempt resources according to the law:

- A home, under specific, limited circumstances. For instance, the house must be a person's primary place of residence. A single person who is going into a nursing home could be required to show an intent to return home, even if it never happens. Make note of the fact that a home is not automatically exempt if a person is single. It is, in fact, at risk of being sold.

- One vehicle

- Burial plots

- Irrevocable prepaid funeral plans

- Life insurance, but only if the face value is $1,500 or less (If it goes over $1,500 in total face value, the cash value in the policy is then considered countable).

- All other resources are most often considered as non-exempt and are countable in regard to financial eligibility. Such resources can include all money and property that can be valued and then converted into cash. These include but are not limited to the following:

- Cash, checking or savings accounts

- Certificates of deposit

- U.S. savings bonds

- Retirement accounts like IRA, 401K, and TSA plans (In a few instances, the community spouse could be exempt).

- Nursing home accounts

- Pre-paid funeral contracts that can be canceled

- Trusts (depending on type of trust and funding date)

- Real estate other than that of the primary residence

- A second car

- Boats or recreational vehicles

- Stocks, bonds, or mutual funds

- Promissory notes

*****

It's no secret that the rules for Medicaid (or honestly anything related to the government) are complicated, but someone who is single will only qualify to receive Medicaid benefits when he or she has less than $2,000 in countable assets. But this is where a legal professional specializing in this area would be greatly beneficial to you or your loved one(s).

*****

MARRIED COUPLES AND MEDICAID ELIGIBILITY

The federal government is not unaware that, for those married couples, having one ill spouse and one healthy one can be detrimental to both. To keep this from happening, there are rules that have been put into place to give additional resources for both care and support of the spouse who is well. This is known as the Community Spouse Resource Allowance (or CSRA).

What this does is it lets the spouse who is well keep one-half of the countable resources with a minimum of $24,180 and a maximum of $120,900. As an example, if a married couple has $25,000 in any countable resources, the amount of the allowance for the community spouse is a *minimum* of $24,180. If said couple has $100,000 in countable resources, that allowance would then be $50,000. If they have $250,000 in countable resources, the allowance then becomes a maximum of $120,900.

It is important to note that the above amounts were effective for the period of time for 2017, and they are updated each year, so next year may be different.

Once any and all exempt resources have been determined and the community spouse resource allowance has been given, any resources that remain are then subject to spend down, which we mentioned earlier.

*****

THE LOOK BACK PERIOD

As you've no doubt noticed and understood, there is a lot that can be easily misunderstood and leave us scratching our heads. When it comes to things like Medicare or Medicaid, or even the government in general, there is so much information that is necessary for us to know. Our goal here, however, is to help you, the reader, to understand these things as easy and painless as possible. We want this to be an enjoyable read so that you can not only make it through the book (because no one likes to read things that are boring), but even more so that you can retain the information you glean from it.

One of those things that many elders and their families often stumble on when trying to understand it is, you guessed it: Medicaid's look back period. It's quite likely you may have *heard* of the look back period, but what *is* it exactly, and how can it affect your or your loved one's eligibility to receive long-term care?

Those are all great and legitimate questions, so let's take some time to answer them for you.

WHAT IS IT?

Basically, Medicaid is designed so that it doesn't start paying for things like long-term care until you can no longer pay for it yourself. As an example, let's say you have several thousand dollars in savings. Well, according to Medicaid, you've got to spend your several thousand dollars before it'll step in to pay for that long-term care for you.

Because of this, a lot of people begin the process of long-term planning in order to keep safe at least a little bit of their savings and assets, so that said assets can go onto help support a spouse or any children, while still also letting them qualify for Medicaid under the program guidelines.

Let's take a look at another quick example. Say that, before you pass away, you want to gift your son or daughter $10,000. That's wonderful, but there's a possibility you might need that $10,000 to help pay for long term care before Medicaid will come in. If you want to keep that money safe, you could go ahead and gift that money to them right now. You can most certainly do that, with caution, however.

You need to be aware of the lookback period. And while it can initially seem confusing, it really isn't all that bad. Basically, the look back period is a five-year period of time in which Medicaid checks out your financial history. They're checking to see if you've made any transfers (or "gifts") of any money or assets.

We'll talk more about gifts and everything that goes with them in more depth in the next chapter. For now, just know that that's what they're looking for. The Medicaid rules regarding giving money away are as follows: in general, any transfer of assets over $500 that is unqualified or uncompensated could end in experiencing a period of ineligibility to receive Medicaid benefits. While the $500 limit is a "general rule," be aware that Medicaid can question any expenditure.

You should also know that that very same "look back" period will be applied to any asset as well—any asset that is either transferred or sold to someone else has to have been done for "fair market value." To help you better understand what we're talking about here, let's say that you sell your house to your sibling for $20,000, but its "fair market value" is actually $100,000. Going by the rules, that transfer was done for *less* than "fair market value."

So, what happens then?

Well, when Medicaid looks and sees that, it's going to be a red flag for them in your financial history. In just such a case, or in any other when there is a transfer or "gift" for less than fair market value, there could be a penalty for the difference in value if it isn't soon corrected. While that may seem to not make much sense, they do have a reason for doing things that way. The main reason for it is simply because they don't want someone who has money and assets to become eligible for Medicaid simply by giving away everything they own to a family member or friend.

This is also the main reason why it's critical to have each and every day of your financial history from the past five years evaluated by a professional. They're equipped with the know-how to find any sort of transaction that could potentially cause an issue with Medicaid before submitting the application. This way, it can get taken care of before it results in a penalty or gets the application denied altogether.

To finish up this particular section before moving on, just remember that the Medicaid look back period is exactly five years from the date of the application to receive benefits, and that any gifts or transfers you make during that period could potentially be subject to a penalty.

*****

QUALIFIED INCOME TRUSTS (QIT)

Also called Miller Trusts, Qualified Income Trusts (or QITs) were put into place by the Omnibus Budget Reconciliation Act of 1993. In New Jersey, they use QITs, but what are they exactly, or what do they do?

Let's find out together…

If the person who is applying for Medicaid eligibility has monthly income that goes beyond the legal amount to receive benefits (as of January 1, 2017, this amount was $2,205.00), then a Qualified Income Trust is necessary, and has to then be created out of the applicant's income in order that he or she could then be eligible to receive long-term nursing home care benefits. As we said, this is sometimes called a Miller Trust, and you should know that it is, in fact, an irrevocable one as well.

So, whatever the amount of the applicant's income that exceeds the eligibility criteria, that is then put into the trust and another person other than the applicant themselves is designated as trustee. But be certain that the entire payor source is placed into trust and not just the amount that exceeds the monthly threshold.

Those persons who might think about using a Qualified Income Trust have to be in need of an institutional level of care and could be residing in a nursing home, an assisted living facility, or their own home. The costs of care will also vary depending on the living arrangements too.

Qualified Income Trusts also have to meet certain conditions, so let's take a look at them now:

- They must only contain the income of the person applying.

- The should NOT contain any resources like income from the sale of either real or personal property or any money from a savings account.

- They have to be irrevocable.

- They need a trustee to manage the administration of the Trust and expenditures from it as stated in both federal and state laws.

- The state of New Jersey must be the first beneficiary when it comes to all remaining funds up to the amount that was paid for Medicaid benefits when the recipient dies.

- Finally, any income that gets put into the QIT must only be used for Post-Eligibility Treatment of Income and also to pay for any costs of care.

QITs will replace the Medically Needy eligibility program that is currently used for nursing facilities. People who get benefits through that program before the date the QIT takes effect will be grandfathered in. You need to be aware, though, that limits for Medicaid eligibility resources will be $2,000 per individual and $3,000 per couple.

While Qualified Income Trusts are normally put into place via a lawyer, the Division of Medical Assistance and Health Services has a template and a set of FAQs that people can use on their own.

Any Qualified Income Trusts that are created for Medicaid recipients must first be approved by the agency that determines eligibility and will then be renewed yearly by the aforementioned Division of Medical Assistance and Health Services.

Any funds that are left after payments are made under Post-Eligibility Treatment of Income have to be kept in the Trust until the beneficiary dies. If it isn't, this can have an effect on the person's eligibility to receive Medicaid benefits.

*****

We've reached the end of another chapter now, and we've covered so much together already, but there's still more to go over.

In the next chapter, we'll be talking more in-depth about gifting, penalties and all that entails.

CHAPTER 3

MEDICAID GIFTING & PENALTIES

It's basically a universal truth that everyone likes receiving gifts. Whether for holidays or birthdays or simply just because, it is a way for us to show our appreciation to and for one another, and each of us has gotten several gifts over the course of our lives from family, friends or coworkers. Now, imagine if those gifts we were given came with some form of penalty.

Hard to imagine, right?

For the elderly among us who have to think about what will happen to their loved ones after they're gone, having something they've given away become penalized is a distinct possibility.

But I'm getting ahead of myself.

First of all, we have to discern the definition of what a gift is when we're referring to Medicaid specifically. We talked earlier about the Medicaid look back period, which is the five-year period in which Medicaid looks into your finances for any type of red flag that might hinder you from receiving Medicaid benefits.

So, a gift, in this sense, would be money, but a gift can be other things as well.

If we think about long and hard enough, we probably all know an older person who tends to be overly generous with his or her money. It could be an older family member, or *we* might be that person ourselves. For the sake of our purposes now, let's say that it's us. If we think we might need or want to apply for Medicaid in order to help with long-term care costs sometime down the road, we're going to want to be careful with just giving our money away freely. Not being careful can have some consequences we may not be aware of at the time.

As we said, according to Medicaid, if you transfer certain assets within a five-year period before you apply to receive those benefits, you'll then be ineligible during that time period—known as a transfer penalty. However, it is dependent on how much money you actually transferred. Keep in mind, though, that even a small transfer can affect your eligibility. In 2017, the IRS regulations allow for up to $14,000 per year as a gift with no reporting requirements and without having to worry about also paying a gift tax. That number could be higher or lower in the future, but Medicaid would still see that gift as a transfer which may result in a penalty.

You should be aware that any kind of transfer you make can be scrutinized by Medicaid. It doesn't matter how you meant it to look, innocent or not, the possibility it will be looked at and potentially flagged is still there. As an example, take charities. If you give some of your money to your favorite charity, even that might negatively affect your eligibility chances to receive Medicaid benefits later on. In the same way, so also can gifts for holidays or weddings, birthdays or graduations. Even buying something for a friend or relative.

Yes, even that.

All these things have the potential to cause a transfer penalty, which can, in turn, affect your chances of being eligible for benefits.

Also, remember that every state is different. If you spend a lot of cash all at once or even over time, you could get something in the mail from the state asking you to verify how you spent the money. If you don't have the correct information or documentation showing that you got fair market value in exchange for the asset you transferred, you might incur a transfer penalty, so it's something to keep in mind.

We'll get more into penalties a little bit later on, though. For now, let's keep talking about gifts. To be more specific, let's talk about the difference between gifting with Medicaid laws vs. gifting with IRS laws.

GIFTING: MEDICAID VS. IRS

As you may know, gifting is a major way that elder law estate planning attorneys can use to help save a client's assets from things like nursing home or long-term care costs, regardless of whether they just want to be proactive and are planning ahead or are in need of Medicaid benefits right now in order that they can pay their nursing home or other care costs. Gifting for the purpose of protecting one's assets is, in fact, presided over by Medicaid law. A lot of people are also aware that they're also able to make gifts under IRS law too, without having to pay a gift tax.

The thing is, Medicaid and the IRS have some very different rules.

Let's take a look.

We've mentioned the five-year look back period a lot now, and we've touched on penalties too. As we said, if you gift during that five-year period, you may incur a penalty period. The reason for this is because any of the money you gifted during that time could have been used to pay for nursing home costs or any kind of long-term care costs. So, since you gave it away instead of using it to pay for those things that you needed, you incurred a penalty instead.

Moving onto the IRS law, you can give up to $14,000 to as many people as you want per year. This is known as an "annual exclusion," and you don't have to file a gift tax return or pay any form of gift tax on it. Along with those gifts, you can also currently give away as much as $5.49 million within your lifetime without either yourself or those who received the gifts having to pay any gift or income taxes on it. If you're feeling incredibly generous and wind up giving more than $14,000 to any person in one year, it will then be necessary for you to file a gift tax return in order to let the IRS know that you have given over the annual exclusion amount in order to see if you reach the $5.49 million gift tax exemption amount.

Now, let's spend some time talking about rules and penalties.

GIFT RULES AND PENALTIES

By this point, we've mentioned penalties several times, and you're more than familiar with how they can happen. However, that doesn't mean there's not still more to say. Before we get there though, let's take a look at some rules.

Rules

So, let's say that you're a nursing home resident. If that was true, then Medicaid does not want you to give away any of your assets to family members in order to hide your true resources. If you want to transfer any property whatsoever, Medicaid wants you to get full value for it in return for the exchange. What this means is that, if you want to leave your house to your children before moving into a nursing home, your children would pay you the fair market value of the house before you go. You are not allowed to just up and *give* them your home or accept any less than the fair market value of the property. That is, unless, you have engaged the services of an experienced elder law attorney who then may be able to provide you with techniques to protect assets even if you are currently in a long term care setting.

That's just how it is.

In order to fight back against people gifting things for the purpose of hiding assets, the Deficit Reduction Act (or DRA) from 2005 upped the strictness of Medicaid's gift-giving rules. That's what it does in a general sense. In a more *specific* sense, it focuses on the transferring of both real estate and any other assets that are owned by nursing home residents. Thanks to this law, any Medicaid recipient who is going into a nursing home and is also looking to Medicaid to cover the entire cost of their stay is then open to having any and all of their property and assets come under review. It's during this time that the look back period we've mentioned so often now is in effect, and anything that got transferred before they applied for nursing home coverage will be looked at.

Any transfer of assets or property for which the resident did not get full market value for will be considered in determining the penalty when trying to apply to receive Medicaid benefits.

Penalties

A potential result of that penalty period we mentioned is being considered as ineligible to receive Medicaid benefits for a pretty substantial period of time. Just how long is determined by adding up the value of any and all property or assets that were given away, and then dividing that number by the average cost of any private nursing home expenses in order to see how many months would have been covered by those benefits.

Basically, what this means is that Medicaid will look at how long you would have been able to pay for nursing home care using that income that you would have received from transferring the asset(s) or property, and then however long that period would have been, that is the length of the penalty period—or, the period of time in which you would be ineligible to receive any benefits from Medicaid.

For a cash gift, normally any amount above $500 may trigger a penalty or if any other assets were sold for less than their fair market value, as we mentioned above. As an example, say that you sell your house for $150,000, but its actual value is $300,000. Since you sold it for less than its full value, the penalty will be the difference between the two that would add up to the full $300,000.

The penalty would then be the remaining $150,000, since that adds up to the full amount.

After that period of ineligibility has passed, you will be able to apply for Medicaid benefits once again. If you made no other transfers during your period of ineligibility, you will be accepted and any nursing home costs will be covered.

It is important to note, however, that you could be considered as ineligible to receive benefits for an indeterminate amount of time depending on the amount of assets transferred or the manner in which you transfer them if you have not engaged in proper planning.

*****

CURING A MEDICAID PENALTY

We've talked at length about penalties already, but how do we go about curing a penalty once we've incurred one? Is that even possible or is it just some sort of pipe dream?

The good news is: It *is*, in fact, possible to cure a Medicaid penalty, so let's see how we do it. In order to do so, we must first calculate a penalty, so we'll just think of a quick example.

Let's say that you are an elderly grandparent with an income of $3,500 a month. You decide you're going to give a gift of $75,000 to a family member. We already know that the length of the penalty period is measured in the number of months you could have paid to receive needed nursing or assisted living care had you not made the gift. In the case of our example, we would take the $75,000 and divide it by the average cost of care per month in our state. In this case, the average cost of care in New Jersey utilized as the divisor is approximately $12,700 a month.

So, $75,000 divided by $12,700 equals 5.9 months.

Thus, the penalty period would last approximately 6 months. During that time, Medicaid would not pay for any type of nursing home or assisted living care, or any home care providers; you would need to find another method of payment.

However, let's say that you exhaust all your assets and are then eligible to qualify for Medicaid benefits. That's great, but because you made the gift of $75,000, you're now looking at that 6 month period of time where Medicaid won't cover you. You have the option of using your income to pay for the care that you need, but if the nursing home costs $12,000, your monthly income won't be enough to cover it.

What do you do then?

The easy solution is to get your family member to begin returning some of the money you gifted in order to pay for your care. If the nursing home costs $12,000, and you have an income of $3,500, that means that your family member will need to return about $8,500 per month. After 6 months has passed, about $51,000 of the total gift will have been returned.

Once the penalty period is passed on the gift, Medicaid will begin paying for the care that you need.

What remains of that $75,000 that wasn't returned belongs to your family member, who can then use those funds to buy things that Medicaid won't cover, like personal items for you. It shouldn't be given back to you though, since that could potentially disqualify you from receiving Medicaid benefits. Whatever money remains with the family member at the time of your death is not subject to Medicaid Recovery.

*****

Now, let's take a look at how to avoid the Medicaid penalty as well as some exceptions to the penalty as well.

AVOIDING THE MEDICAID PENALTY

I know that it likely doesn't seem that there's any light at the end of the tunnel so to speak, but the good news is that there are, in fact, multiple techniques and exceptions to these rules and exemptions that can be made for those families who find themselves between a rock and a hard place. Under the rules established by these exceptions, Medicaid applicants are able to transfer assets to certain individuals during the look back period without running the risk of being penalized for it.

See? There *is* a silver lining after all. However, while that is quite fortunate indeed, less so is the fact that these options can be and are sometimes confusing and hard to put into place without the aid of someone like a professional elder law attorney well versed in Medicaid law.

LOOK BACK: EXCEPTIONS AND EXEMPTIONS

Spouses

As of this year, an applicant's spouse is allowed to retain 50% of the assets of the couple up to a maximum of $120,900, if that spouse was not also applying for Medicaid themselves and would continue to live independently of the other. To put it another way, the spouse who is *not* applying for Medicaid benefits can keep up to $120,900 of the couple's assets. This is known as the Community Spouse Resource Allowance, which we mentioned previously. The titling of the account is irrelevant so total resources are counted whether titled jointly or to each spouse separately. You should be aware that the dollar amount can change from year to year and there are some variables to this exception depending on what state you live in.

Each state is either a 50% state or a 100% state. This means that the spouse who isn't applying for Medicaid benefits (aka: the Community Spouse) is able to keep up to either 50% or 100% of the assets. What remains of the assets is then "spent down" to help with the cost of nursing home care until the person who actually needs that care can meet the asset limit and thus qualify to receive benefits.

Disabled Children

People applying to receive Medicaid benefits can either transfer assets to or establish trusts for any disabled children or children under the age of 21. This also includes any children who are legally blind.

Siblings

A home can be transferred to a sibling if that sibling owns at least a portion of the home (that is, they have equity in the home) and they have to have lived there for at least a year before the applicant was placed in a nursing home or assisted living facility.

Adult Children Caregivers

An exemption known as the "Child Caregiver Exemption" is made for those adult children who live with the Medicaid applicant (i.e. their parents) and who also are their primary caregivers. Under this rule, the parent may transfer the home to the child without any fear of penalty if the child lived with the parent for a 2 year period prior to entry into a long term care facility and provided a level of care to the parent that kept them out of the facility for that period of time.

Debt Payments

If you pay off any debts you have while you're in the look back period, those are also exempt from causing a violation. As an example, you could pay off your mortgage or home equity line of credit. In fact, doing so is a fantastic way to turn any countable liquid assets into exempt ones.

*****

COMMON MISTAKES AND VIOLATIONS

While we're on the subject, it might behoove us to take a quick look at some of the common mistakes and violations that people make, so let's take time and do that now.

Gifts

Because the federal government allows any U.S. citizen to gift money (as much as $5.49 million as of this year) thanks to the estate and gift tax exemption without having to pay tax on it, a lot of people might not know that Medicaid doesn't consider it to be exempt from the look back period. Even those gifts we make for special occasions, like holidays, weddings, or birthdays, could result in a penalty by Medicaid. This is also true of any charitable donations we might make. What makes things even harder is that the rules for gifting vary according to state.

Lack of Documentation

Even if you happen to sell an asset and get a value that is equal to its fair market value, it could still result in a violation if you don't have the proper paperwork to back up the transaction. This applies particularly to those assets that the government keeps a record on, such as boats, motorcycles, or vehicles via registrations.

Irrevocable Trusts

A lot of people incorrectly assume that an irrevocable trust (also known as a Medicaid Qualifying Trust) is exempt from the look back period. While you might think that it is, it is, unfortunately, not. As you're probably aware, a trust is a form of legal arrangement where a person (known as the grantor) transfers assets and ownerships to a third party (known as the trustee). The trustee will then hold the assets for the beneficiary. The kinds of assets that can be transferred include the following:

- Stocks

- CDs

- Annuities

- Cash

- Property

In the case of an irrevocable trust, the grantor is unable to change or revoke the trust (as the name implies). A revocable trust, however, *can* be changed. Any irrevocable trusts that are made during the look back period are then considered to be gifts and, because of this, are in violation of the look back period—thus incurring a penalty. You should be aware that any irrevocable trusts made *before* the look back period are not considered to be assets.

Strategies for Avoiding Penalties

In this chapter all about penalties, it would be a great disservice to you, the reader, if we did not spend the closing pages discussing ways to actually *avoid* those penalties. We've talked about nearly everything else related to them, and it is good information, certainly. But what if we want to simply avoid even the *chance* of accruing a penalty?

How do we do that?

First and foremost, there is good news: there are strategies that you can use to help your family or loved ones to keep at least a portion of their assets or even achieve eligibility for Medicaid benefits. And while the strategies below can certainly be of assistance, you should still seek the help and advice of a professional in this field, as these can definitely be rather complex and you want to do whatever it takes to help rectify the situation.

With that said, let's look at the strategies.

*****

1. Caregiver and Lease Agreements

Caregiver agreements may also be referred to by another, similar name: life care agreements, elder contracts or long-term personal supports services agreements. Regardless of their name, they are contracts that set forth the caregiving relationship between an elderly person and his or her caregiving relative. It is a formal agreement that lets seniors reimburse the relative for the care provided as well as "spend down" their assets without causing a violation of the Medicaid look back period. They also let the elder get the care he or she needs that Medicaid doesn't cover, while still giving their family members the compensation they need too. You should be aware that these contracts can remain effective even when the elderly person has gone into a nursing home facility, and the caregiver themselves has become the elder's advocate.

It is also incredibly important that the document be drafted very carefully, and should include the date that services first began, as well as the responsibilities of the caregiver, no matter if it's shopping for essential items, transportation, preparing meals, or even help with personal care. It should also include the hours that the caregiver will work, and the caregiver must keep a careful log of all their duties they carry out, their daily hours, and keep written invoice of all services rendered.

The contract must also state the amount to be compensated (which should be reasonable when compared to the services provided) to the caregiver in return for any duties or services they provide for the elder.

Lease agreements are also very important if the parent is paying a child or another relative to live in child's home. A lease agreement will show fair market value is being received in exchange for the payment.

2. Medicaid Exempt Annuities

Annuities, which are also known as Medicaid Annuities or Medicaid Compliant Annuities, are a tried and true method for avoiding violation of the look back period. When it comes to an annuity, a person will pay one lump sum in cash in return for receiving monthly payments for the duration of their own life or the life of their spouse, or for a predetermined number of years. These annuities are compliant with Medicaid because they change assets into income, which works to lower the assets that the applicant has to an amount that is less than the limit for Medicaid eligibility. It should also be said that getting an annuity during the look back period is also not in violation of those rules. With that said, however, the rules for this vary from state to state regarding Medicaid annuities and those who benefit from them. There are also no small numbers of ill-informed annuity salespeople who won't necessarily know about how well their product is compliant with Medicaid rules. Be extremely careful.

Deferring annuities is **not** a strategy for avoiding violation of the look back rule, however. This is because that any deferred payments that an investor sets aside for a specific time could be used to pay for the costs of any long-term care.

Utilizing annuities in a spousal situation or an annuity in conjunction with a trust are great techniques in protecting assets if that is a goal of the elder.

3. Undue Hardship Waiver

Like its name implies, an Undue Hardship Waiver allows the Medicaid Penalty Period to be waived completely. As an example, if someone violates the look back period but will, as a result, be without his or her basic needs—like food, water, shelter, etc.—then he or she is able to request an Undue Hardship Waiver. However, he or she has to try all other methods for recovering any transferred assets. This includes legal options too. It needs to be said, though, that it can be very hard getting an Undue Hardship Waiver, so it's probably best not to need it in the first place.

4. Professional Medicaid Planning Assistance

Dealing with Medicaid's look back period is very confusing and there are a lot steps involved. We've seen a lot of good examples of how to go about it, but the best way to avoid violating it and thus incurring all that comes with doing so is to talk with a Medicaid planner before you gift or transfer any assets. The planner will be able to give you help even if you *have* violated the look back period and thus have a penalty that would render you ineligible to receive the help you need from Medicaid.

*****

Once you've recovered from the massive amount of information found in this chapter, we'll take you all the way back to the beginning of the process and see how exactly we go about starting the Medicaid application process and what all we can expect during it.

CHAPTER 4

THE MEDICAID APPLICATION PROCESS

We've covered a great deal about Medicaid already, and to be honest, we could fill *several* books full of information on the things we've covered in each of these chapters. Our goal, though, is not simply to overwhelm, but to educate. We want to help you figure out exactly what you need to know, but we want to do it in a way that is easy to understand and enjoyable to read. After all, if something isn't enjoyable, why read it, right?

Right.

So, with that said, we hope that this journey so far has been both entertaining and informative.

In this chapter, as you've seen, we'll be discussing what all goes into the application process for Medicaid, and we have a lot of sections we want to get through, so let's not waste any time and jump right in.

*****

WHAT DO I NEED?

When you go to apply for nearly anything at all, you must first prove that you are, in fact, who you say you are. It is no different when you apply for something like Medicaid. When you begin the application process, you'll need to show them not only who you are, but also where you live, what you own, how much money you get in a month, where you get it from, and how much of that money you spend on things like living expenses.

So, let's break it down so it's a bit easier to wrap our minds around. We'll start from the beginning—always a good spot.

Who are you?

First things first: as we said, you're going to have to show them that you are the person you claim to be—and not only your identity, but your age, citizenship and marital status as well. Let's take a look at some documents that will help you in each category:

Identity

- U.S. Passport
- Driver's License
- State issued I.D.
- Voter Registration Card
- Work or School I.D.
- Clinic or Medical Card
- Medicare Card

Age

- U.S. Passport
- Birth Certificate

- Driver's License
- Baptismal Certificate

Citizenship

- U.S. Passport
- Birth Certificate
- Naturalization Papers
- Alien Registration Card

Marital Status

- Marriage License
- Divorce Decree
- Death Certificate
- Separation Papers

Where do you live?

After you've shown them who you are, you're going to have to show them where you live. For our purposes here, we'll say New Jersey, but any of the following can apply to your own state as well:

- Copy of Deed to Home
- Rent Receipt
- Apartment Lease
- Current Utility Bill
- NJ Driver's License
- Statement from Landlord

What do you own?

A great many people don't realize just how much they actually own. When you think of owning something, most often our minds go to *big* things, such as homes or cars. But in reality, it can include a great deal of smaller things as well. In order for Medicaid to have a crystal-clear picture of your current financial standing, you're going to need copies of a lot of different documents. Those include:

- Deeds to any owned property

- Any Certificates of Deposit

- Pre-paid funeral arrangements

- Annuities

- IRAs

- Other Vehicles (like a boat, trailer, etc.)

- Mobile Home

- Any property tax statements

- Any and all life insurance policies

- Trusts or any other holding instruments

- 401k/403b retirement accounts

- Mortgages

- Christmas or Vacation Club accounts

- Any business or real estate partnership papers

- Stocks or Bonds

- Deeds to any burial plots

- Any special needs trust

- Keogh Accounts

- Any vehicle registrations

- Burial Accounts

*****

I know that was a lot, but would you believe there's even more? In addition to what we listed above, you're also going to need the last sixty months' worth of statements for any and all financial accounts that were opened or closed over the past five years. You'll also be required to show any financial passbooks from accounts like:

- Checking accounts

- Money Market Accounts

- Savings accounts

- Any transfers of either money or real estate

- Any credit union shares or accounts

*****

How much do you make?

While most all of us don't like talking about how much money we do or don't have, you're going to *need* to talk about it if you're looking to apply for Medicaid benefits. You'll need to show proof of your monthly income, and it can be earned—as in getting a paycheck, or unearned, if you happen to receive interest from any investment accounts you have. Also note that **if you had to file any federal income tax returns you have to bring in copies of them with any and all attached schedules, over the past 5 years.** Some examples of documents that can prove how much income you have each month can be seen below.

It's also important to remember that any and all applicants have to give their Social Security card and Medicare card too.

- Any most recent pay stubs

- Any support or alimony payments

- Unemployment check stub

- Dividend checks

- Self-employment statement

- VA check stub

- SSI payments

- Worker's Compensation check stub

- Income statement from employer

- Social Security check stub

- Temporary Disability check stub

What are your living expenses?

The next thing you're going to need to prove is how much money it costs per month for you to live. A substantial part of your monthly income can go toward upkeep on your house or renting an apartment. Let's take a look at some of the documents you can give to the Board of Social Services worker helping you are as follows:

- Rent receipts

- Telephone bills

- Water or sewer bill

- Health insurance bills

- Mortgage statements

- Gas/oil bill

- Installation/connection charges

- Unpaid medical bills

- Real estate tax bills

- Electric bill

- Renter or home owner insurance

- Any outstanding loans

Keep in mind that these are only a few of the things you can use; they aren't all of them. And while the Board of Social Services may use flat allowances on some items, it's best to know what your monthly expenses consist of.

Along with all of the documents in the categories we listed above, you're also going to need to bring any documents that show that you have designated a **POWER OF ATTORNEY** or **THIRD PARTY SIGNATOR** who has also signed an Authorized Representative form in order to help you with your finances and application. It is also possible that you could be asked to give information more than what we've already shown. The reason for this is because you want to be sure that your Board of Social Services has the best possible understanding of your specific situation as possible. It isn't just them working for you; rather, it is you working together to help provide the best care possible for your own unique situation.

If you're applying on behalf of someone who is incapacitated and unable to apply for themselves, you're also going to need to include any documentation that shows **GUARDIANSHIP** as well.

*****

What Can I Expect?

Now that we've seen all the paperwork and documentation you'll need when applying for Medicaid, what comes next? What can you expect once everything gets going?

Let's take a look.

So, after you've gotten together everything you're going to need and have everything in order, a caseworker will then be assigned to your specific case and will proceed to go over all the documents that you have submitted to Medicaid. Be aware that caseworkers are often overworked and understaffed, and they might see dozens of applications per week, depending on the area, so it could take a while to get to you.

Patience *is* a virtue after all.

As long you do your best to ensure that your application is both clear and precise, and you remember to include ALL the correct documentation, and if it is evident that you *do* qualify, it will help the caseworker in processing your application.

Conversely, if the application and all documents aren't structured, prepared or presented in a way that makes it clear and easy to read and understand, your application could get thrown on a "get to later" pile. This has the potential to delay your approval by several months. What's more—if the person in charge of handling the application isn't aware of all the complexity that comes along with Medicaid eligibility and any mistakes are made, the caseworker could even impose a penalty on the application or simply deny it altogether.

That's why it's so important to have everything in order the first time so that you don't have to deal with headaches later on. And that's where hiring a professional to help you can work wonders.

*****

WHERE DO I APPLY?

The good news here is that, for those living in New Jersey, there are three main ways to go about applying for Medicaid. Those are:

• Online application

- Personal application

- Application via telephone

Online Application

The most popular form of application for children and families seeking NJ FamilyCare/Medicaid in New Jersey is done via online. The first step you'll want to take is using the State's online self-screening tool, known as NJHelps. It can be found by accessing the following link: www.njhelps.org.

Using this tool will help you to figure out whether or not you'll actually qualify for Medicaid in New Jersey and will list the documents you'll need to give them if you wish to apply for the program, which we've already covered above. Once you've passed the online screening tool, you can then go and download an online application form by using the following link:
 http://www.njfamilycare.org.

Personal Application

If you choose to apply in person, you can do so by visiting your county's board of social services. If you'd like to know more about the locations you can visit when making a personal application, you can do so by going online to
http://www.state.nj.us/humanservices/dfd/programs/njsnap/cwa.

When you visit one of the offices listed on the website above, you'll find a qualified staff member who will work with you to apply for the NJ Medicaid program by evaluating you for any and all types of Medicaid or any other assistance programs that may be offered by the State. You need to be aware that an appointment is necessary before heading to the county board to receive any services.

Phone Application

You could also simply choose to apply for Medicaid over the phone if you cannot do it online or in person. There are a variety of numbers available to call depending on your preferred location too. Some of them include:

- **(609) 348-3001 (Atlantic County)**

- **(856) 225-8800 (Camden County)**

- **(732) 745-3500 (Middlesex County)**

*****

Once you've been deemed as eligible to receive Medicaid, there are still a few more general eligibility requirements you'll have to meet, such as:

- You must be a citizen of the United States or qualified alien.

- You have to be a resident of the State of New Jersey (to apply for NJ Medicaid).

- You'll also need to meet specific standards for your financial assets and income.

- As discussed previously, you may be able to receive NJ Medicaid retroactively.

New Jersey Medicaid Retroactive Eligibility

All this means is that eligibility to receive New Jersey Medicaid retroactive eligibility is backdated to any or all three months prior to the date of application. What this means, then, is that Medicaid coverage will stop at the end of the month in which a person's circumstances change.

*****

If you've made it this far, you're halfway through the chapter, and you've made it through a lot of information already. With that said, there's still more to get through.

In the second half, we'll take a look at the following three areas:

- When you should apply for Medicaid

- Redeterminations after you've been approved, and,

- How to get help if you need it.

So, without further ado, let's jump right in.

WHEN SHOULD I APPLY?

So, now we know more about what to expect during the application process, and about the process in general, but *when* exactly would be the right time to apply? After all, you don't want to apply too early, but neither do you want to apply too late.

Is there a "too late" when it comes to applying for Medicaid? There are a lot of questions surrounding this subject, and it can be quite confusing, so let's answer it now.

The truth is that the best time to apply for Medicaid is dependent on a number of factors—things like your medical situation, marital status, and how complex your finances are. If things are fairly straightforward with regard to your finances, the state could process your application more quickly. If you're in need of long-term care, you should make it a point to apply as soon as you possibly can, since it can potentially be a while before the state will be able to process your application and determine your eligibility status. Generally, the date that you become eligible for Medicaid benefits is based on the date which you applied—this assumes you meet all the eligibility requirements when you put in the application. So, the longer that you put off applying, the later your eligibility date is going to be.

Normally, the Medicaid agency is allowed up to **45 days to process an application**. If a determination of disability is necessary, it can take up to 90 days, but it could take some more time for the state to determine your eligibility status if you don't have the proper documents on time. If the Medicaid agency thinks of you as being uncooperative, it can then deny your eligibility for failing to cooperate. If this occurs, you may possibly have to restart the application process once you have the needed documentation. Doing so would then delay your eligibility date for an even longer period.

If they deem you as eligible to receive benefits, however, you will then receive a letter that includes the **date of eligibility and the amount you have to pay toward the cost of care**. This is considered to be your share of the cost.

Medicaid will then review your eligibility status yearly. During this review, you might be required to document both your income and assets once more. This is especially true if either your income or assets have gone through many changes (or changed at all) over the course of the last year. Generally, this process tends to be much simpler as opposed to the original application process.

If you are deemed as ineligible, you will also receive a letter, but this one will explain the reason for your denial. It will also explain to you how you can go about appealing the process.

In the simplest of terms, you just want to make sure that you have everything in order and all your ducks in a row before setting out to begin your journey of receiving Medicaid benefits.

We're coming up on the end of the chapter, but we have two more sections to cover before we get there. To finish up, we will be taking a look at the following:

- **Medicaid Redeterminations after Approval**

- **How to Get Help**

Let's do this!

*****

REDETERMINATIONS AFTER APPROVAL

We've talked about this previously, but you need to remember that even if you are approved to receive Medicaid benefits, Medicaid will review your eligibility status each year.

Now, you might be thinking, "Well, I got it once, why on earth do I need to be reviewed?"

That's a legitimate question, and a good one, and lucky for us, there's a simple answer to it. Simply put, you'll be reviewed because your status might have changed. Your income may have increased, for instance. And as we've already said, one of the eligibility requirements to be able to receive benefits is to fall below a certain amount.

Of course, there are other reasons unrelated to income as well, such as your living arrangements or changes in your resources. All of these things can affect your eligibility, and it's so important that you work to make sure you comply with the redeterminations by Medicaid and the Supplemental Security Income offices. Failure to comply could mean that any benefits you are currently receiving could either be suspended for a time or even terminated altogether. That's why it's so important to get help with the application process, so that the whole thing goes as smoothly and painlessly as it possibly can.

But where do you go for help?

Keep reading.

HOW TO GET HELP

As we said, it can be, and is, a very confusing process trying to figure out the Medicaid application(s) and all things related to it. It would be greatly beneficial to you to seek out the professional help of an Elder Care lawyer. They are well-versed in everything related to elders and their care, as well as any issues they may face and how to best deal with situations that can arise.

This includes Medicaid overall, and the application process specifically. So, make sure to talk to one as soon as possible.

You'll be glad you did.

*****

In the next chapter, we'll be taking a look at the appeals process, and we'll cover the areas of a fair hearing (otherwise known as state court) and federal court as well.

CHAPTER 5

MEDICAID APPEALS

If someone is convicted of a crime, they are taken to court with the intention by the prosecution of being found guilty of committing whatever crime it was. But what does the potentially guilty party do? Of course, while the opposition is busy presenting evidence and trying to get a guilty verdict, the person in question is with his or her defense team trying to prove the opposite—they're trying to prove their client's innocence.

And how do they do that?

By appealing to the judge and jury.

The defense team spends countless hours and no doubt many sleepless nights pouring over the case files looking for anything and everything that might help their client escape a potentially gruesome fate. And sometimes, all that hard work and effort pays off, and they're able to secure a win for not only their client but themselves as well.

Of course, there are also times where it *doesn't* pay off and the client winds up still having to face his or her fate, whatever it may be.

On a different, but yet still similar note, we can go through all the time and effort and hard work of filling out all the forms to apply to receive Medicaid benefits. We can jump through all the hoops and dot all of the I's and cross all the T's, and still sometimes we can face the denial of our application. All that hard work, seemingly for nothing.

Or is it?

You see, if your application does, in fact, get denied, it isn't simply the end of the road; you have options available to you.

You can choose to appeal the decision.

For this chapter, we *will* be focusing on the issue of Medicaid appeals, and we'll look at two distinct areas: fair hearings (also known as state hearings) and federal court hearings.

Let's continue on.

*****

FAIR HEARINGS (STATE HEARINGS)

To begin, you should know that there are, in fact, a number of reasons why an applicant for Medicaid may find themselves in the position to have a fair hearing. But what exactly *is* a fair hearing anyway? Simply put, a fair hearing is one that takes place before an administrative law judge. If you apply for Medicaid and are not then satisfied with the decision of the Board of Social Services, you have a right to a fair hearing as the beginning of the appeal process.

As an example, let's say that you think that you get approved for Medicaid benefits, but the Board of Social Services states that your coverage will begin in April, while you think it should begin in January. You then have the option to request a fair hearing.

If Medicaid deems an applicant as ineligible because he or she gave away $50,000 in gifts but you don't think the applicant gave away anything, you may request a fair hearing for the applicant.

Likewise, if Medicaid says that you need to pay the nursing facility $1,000 a month from your income when you're on Medicaid, but you require that money for your spouse or for some other medical expense, you can then ask for a fair hearing.

As you can see, there are many, many reasons why you or someone else might wish to ask for a fair hearing.

However, you'll want to be quick about it if you do. You are required to write to Medicaid no later than 20 days after receiving the initial decision to obtain a fair hearing. Once you file, they will give you a date and place in which you are to appear. If, for some reason, something comes up and you have very good reason *not* to appear, you must call the person working on your case and request an "adjournment" from them. Then you must call the court—the number should be on the paper you get that lists the date of your hearing—and let them know why you require a new date, and that the caseworker agreed to a new date as well.

As you no doubt have noticed, a Fair Hearing is a type of trial. You will be required to present any and all evidence you have in order to prove that the decision the caseworker made was incorrect. You'll also need to make legal arguments that work to support your position on your eligibility for benefits too, so be prepared for that.

While a Fair Hearing may be a type of trial, there *are* some differences between a Medicaid fair hearing and a regular trial in Superior Court. The main difference between the two is that in a fair hearing, the judge isn't the one making the final decision. Instead, that rests with the Director of the New Jersey Division of Medical Assistance and Health Services (DMAHS). He or she reviews all of the initial decisions and then will either approve the decision, reverse it, or send all parties back to the judge for more facts.

You should also be aware that a fair hearing is no quick affair; they can take quite a long time. The first decision could take up to six months to receive, and then the DMAHS has 45 days to approve or deny the decision. Most generally, they often ask for and receive that 45-day extension. This entire process—from filing for the hearing to getting the final decision—is all considered to be a part of the Medicaid application and nursing facilities cannot discharge any resident while the application is pending.

Any Final Agency Decisions may be appealed to the Superior Court-Appellate Division, or possibly even Federal Court, depending on what the issue is.

Next, let's take a look at some frequently asked questions in regard to fair hearings.

*****

FREQUENTLY ASKED QUESTIONS

1. What are some of the reasons I might need a Fair Hearing?

- You have applied for Medical Assistance as a disabled person, and over 90 days have passed. You have not been told yet if the application is approved or denied.

- You have been told that, due to abuse of Medical Assistance, you have to get medical care from one main provider (Recipient Restriction Program) and you do not agree with the decision.

- You are getting Medical Assistance, but have to pay part of the cost and think your share is too much.

- You are receiving Medical Assistance and have a Managed Care Plan and disagree with the decision about your health benefits or services that were decided for you under the plan.

2. Are there time limits for receiving a Fair Hearing?

- Yes, there are, in fact, time limits. It's best to request a hearing ASAP. If you take too long, you may not be able to get one.

- You can ask for a Fair Hearing within **20-60** days of being notified that your Public Assistance or Medical Assistance has been denied, or will be stopped or reduced depending on the type of Medicaid you are seeking.

- If you receive a notice stating that your Supplemental Nutrition Assistance Program (SNAP) benefits are denied, you can request a Fair Hearing within **90** days of getting the notice. You can also request a hearing if you think you aren't getting enough SNAP benefits anytime within the period of certification. If you appeal within 15 days of the date of the notice, you can get SNAP during the appeal.

- **Look at the notice to be sure of time limits. The notice will specify your time limit.**

- **IF YOU DON'T GET A NOTICE ABOUT YOUR CASE**, and money or services, or any other help is denied, stopped or reduced, you may ask for a Fair Hearing.

3. How will I know if my benefits will continue?

You will receive notification that will confirm your request for a hearing as well as let you know if your benefits will or won't continue while you are waiting for the decision from the Fair Hearing.

4. How will I know when my hearing is scheduled?

The Office of Administrative Hearings will send out notice (OAH-457) that will let you know when and where your hearing will be. If the hearing has been scheduled, you may also get this information via calling 1 (800) 342-3334, and follow the prompts given. In many cases, hearings are scheduled 3-4 weeks after they are requested.

5. What happens if I have an emergency?

If you are in an emergency situation—facing homelessness, eviction, fuel or utility cut-off, etc. or if you have been denied emergency assistance, make that known at the time you request the hearing. In cases like these, the hearing will be scheduled and a decision made ASAP.

6. What if I am disabled and unable to attend a Fair Hearing?

If you are disabled and can't travel you can appear through a representative—either a friend, relative or lawyer. If your representative is not a lawyer or an employee of one, then the representative must bring the hearing office a written letter that you have signed saying that you want them to represent you. If you don't have a representative available and want to participate in the hearing directly, a telephone hearing can be scheduled for you. Medical documentation will be necessary that states you can't travel to the regular meeting location. When you go to request a hearing, you should state in the letter or fax that you are disabled, or tell the interviewer directly. You'll then be told where to turn in medical documentation and about telephone hearing procedures.

7. How do I get ready for my Fair Hearing?

It is your right to look at your case record and to get free copies of all forms and papers which your local agency will give to the Administrative Law Judge at the hearing. You can use these to help you better prepare for the hearing itself. You can also ask for free copies of any other papers that are in your case record that you think you might need at the hearing. You should receive the documents soon after you ask for them, but no later than the time of the hearing.

8. Who will be at the Fair Hearing?

Someone from the local social services agency will attend the Fair Hearing in order to explain the decision regarding your case. Either you or your representative can question him or her and present your side of the case. You or your representative will also have the ability to question any witnesses which you may choose to bring to help your case. As we mentioned previously, the Administrative Law Judge will listen to the testimony and collect evidence, and the hearing will be recorded.

9. What should I bring to the Fair Hearing?

Make it a point to bring with you your scheduling notice, as well as any witnesses you might have and any information that might relate to the hearing, such as:

- Paystubs

- Bills

- Doctor's statements

- Rent receipts

- Photo ID

9. When and how will I get a decision?

A written decision on your hearing will be mailed to you sometime after your hearing has been completed.

10. What happens if the decision says I won my hearing?

- If the decision shows you won the Fair Hearing and your local social services agency is directed to take a certain action, the agency should do this ASAP.

- If you don't think that the agency has taken the action the decision tells it to within a reasonable amount of time after the decision is received, you can submit a Compliance Compliant to the Office of Temporary and Disability

Assistance, and they will then investigate.

- However, if you did not win the hearing, you can bring an appeal in the State Appeals court. If you want to do that and don't know how to go about it, you can contact any legal resources you have available to you, such as the County Bar Association, Legal Aid, Legal Services, etc. You are required to begin the appeal process within a fixed time after the date of the decision from your hearing.

- Keep in mind that these are just a few of the questions you might have regarding fair hearings. We could fill several chapters with questions, but we have so much more to cover. Our intention with these questions is just to give you an idea of some things you might want to ask about should you find yourself in a situation where you need a fair hearing.

*****

FEDERAL COURT

You also have the option to bring suit in Federal Court rather than proceeding down the State route. However, again, this is dependent on what the issue you're trying to appeal is and the author would suggest you contact a seasoned attorney to assist in this type of appeal as the Federal rules can be very complicated and strict.

*****

The topic of Estate Recovery is also important when it comes to discussions on Medicaid, and we will be focusing on just exactly that and all that it entails in the next chapter.

CHAPTER 6

ESTATE RECOVERY

In doing your own research of the Medicaid program and seeking assistance, it's quite likely you may have heard of the term "estate recovery" before. But perhaps you haven't; maybe this chapter right here is your first exposure to the term and you're now scratching your head trying to figure out what it is and what it means.

If so, have no fear. This chapter, as you can see, is all about estate recovery, and if you're just starting out on a journey to educate yourself about a particular thing, the best first step to take would be to define exactly what that thing you're researching actually is.

So, let's begin this chapter with a question and a definition, then.

WHAT IS ESTATE RECOVERY?

According to both federal and New Jersey state law, the Division of Medical Assistance and Health Services (DMAHS) is required to take back funds from the estates of particular deceased clients who received medical help or former clients for any and all payments that were given through Medicaid for any services that were received either on or after the age of 55. In layman's terms, they basically need to recoup the money they spent.

So, then, what exactly *is* an estate?

It's likely that you've heard the term "estate" before, but a refresher is always good.

An estate is simply anything that belonged to a deceased person at the time they passed away. They can include things like:

- The decedent's home or their share of the home

- Any bank accounts (no matter if they're solely or jointly held)

- Trusts and annuities

- Stocks and bonds

*****

According to New Jersey, an estate can be defined as any other real or personal property, as well as any assets in which the deceased person had any sort of legal title or interest at the time they died. This includes assets that are conveyed to any survivor, heir, or assign of the person through things like joint tenancy, tenancy in common, survivorship, living trust, or any other type of similar arrangement.

Even if the property or the share of the property can go to the survivor(s), it's still considered as part of the estate specifically for estate recovery in New Jersey.

Any proceeds from any life insurance policies, however, are considered to be the assets of those beneficiaries who are named. They will only be considered recoverable only when they are paid to the client's estate as the named beneficiary.

Above, we talked about some of the things that we mean when we're talking about an "estate." And if we talked about some of the things that an estate includes, it would also be prudent to talk about those things that it does not include as well.

An estate does **NOT** include the following:

1. A life estate that expires at the time of death

2. An inter vivos trust that is put in place by a third-party for the benefit of the Medicaid beneficiary, given that the person cannot compel distribution and no assets from the trust were owned in the five-year period between the person's application to receive Medicaid benefits and their death.

3. A testamentary trust put into place via a third party, given the Medicaid beneficiary is unable to compel distribution and no assets from the trust were owned in the five years between application for Medicaid and the person's death.

*****

Any lien that has been filed by the DMAHS is a preferred claim against that Medicaid recipient's estate. Keep in mind, though, that the state of New Jersey will not put on a lien or seek to recover (with the exception of any benefits that have been incorrectly or illegally paid) if one of the following occurs:

- There is a surviving spouse

- There is a surviving child younger than the age of 21

- There is a surviving child who is blind or otherwise permanently or totally disabled.

So, with all that said, are you in danger of the state seeking recovery right as soon as someone passes away?

The short answer to that question is simply: yes. If the person in question has no surviving spouse, nor children under 21, or no child who is blind or otherwise permanently or completely disabled—as we mentioned before—they will move into recovery mode.

However, there *are* three times in which recovery would not be pursued. It will not be pursued if:

1. It would not be cost-effective to do so; or

2. Property in the estate is the only source of income for one or more of the survivors, and pursuing recovery would result in one or more of those survivors becoming eligible to receive public assistance and/or Medicaid benefits; or

3. A family member of the deceased has, before they passed away, continued to live in a home owned by the client at the time of the client's death, and that home was his or her primary residence, and was, and remains, the family member's primary residence too. The Division might record a lien against the property, but it will not enforce it until the property is either sold off voluntarily or the resident family member either dies or leaves.

*****

Also, the State will not try to recover anything if there is either a spouse or child that survives, and that child is under 21 or is blind or permanently and totally disabled. In that kind of situation, recovery would be postponed until the child turned 21, or either the spouse or child dies.

We briefly mentioned about liens a minute ago, but what *is* a Medicaid lien?

Basically, a lien is a type of charge or claim that the Department of Social Services puts on your property for the purpose of paying for the Medicaid assistance they pay on your behalf.

Upon application to receive Medicaid benefits, a lien is **NOT** filed against the property. Instead, a lien is put into place only after the Medicaid recipient dies, or death of a former client who received services on or after the age of 55 if there is no surviving spouse, no child under 21, or no child who is blind or otherwise permanently disabled.

The amount that is claimed as a lien will equal the amount of **all** assistance given by DMAHS to the Medicaid recipient for those services they received on or after age 55. This includes any capitation payments that were made to an HMO on behalf of the client by Medicaid.

So, you might be wondering whether or not any type of expenses can be paid by using the assets from the deceased before having to pay Medicaid. If so, you might be interested to know that there *are* some expenses, in fact. Things like reasonable funeral costs and expenses that are related to the administration of the estate. Also, included are any debts that may be owed to the Office of the Public Guardian for Elderly Adults. Next is the claim by DMAHS, along with any debts and taxes with preference under either federal or New Jersey law.

The following things are required with regard to collection procedures and notice:

1. The estate's personal representative must let the State of New Jersey know, in writing, that the Medicaid beneficiary has died and request a payoff statement.

2. A claim or lien must be filed by the appropriate agency against the beneficiary's estate no more than 90 days after they get actual written notice of death.

3. The State of New Jersey has to give the personal representative a payoff statement with the total funds that were expended by the State on behalf of the Medicaid beneficiary up through the date of death—if that information is available. If it is not, then it must be as soon as it is administratively feasible. The representative will then pay an equal amount out of the estate's assets that is equal to the total amount of funds expended via the State.

4. The only action required by New Jersey is to that extent that is necessary for filing a claim or lien against the estate, as well

as set the amount that is to be repaid to the State for any and all funds used by the state on the beneficiary's behalf.

*****

For New Jersey, estate recovery includes any and all payments for services rendered, not only those for beneficiaries who have been institutionalized. Estates of those who are deceased who were also enrolled in any Waiver Programs are subject to recovery as well.

Now, I know what you're thinking. I mean, this is all well and good and it's great to know, but *why*, right? What's the point of all this information?

Admittedly, it's a lot. It's a lot to wrap your mind around and a lot to digest. The goal of this book, as we said before, is simply to be informative, and to be so in a format that is easily understood. That way, you get access to the information you need and your brain won't have to explode trying to decipher what it is we're talking about.

With that said, we're going to switch gears a bit and give you a bit of history on the topic of estate recovery so that you can better get an idea of the *why* of everything.

*****

HISTORY

If we're going to talk a bit of history, it's best, then, to start at the beginning. And since the Medicaid program began all the way back in 1965, all the states have been allowed to recover from estates of those recipients of Medicaid who have passed on. But only as long as they were over the age of 55 when they received their benefits and had no surviving spouse, minor child, or no disabled adult child. In fact, there were twelve states that had some type of estate recovery program up and running before 1990, and this was based on Medicaid's original law. And even though some of these earlier programs had features that have since been documented, things like their scope and the impact on Medicaid recipients—especially when they compare to those states without those early programs—have not been recorded.

Following reports that said estate recovery programs were a cost-effective way to offset any state and/or federal costs, while also promoting more unbiased treatment of Medicaid recipients, Congress was prompted to create a provision in the Omnibus Budget Reconciliation Act of 1993 that required the states to start a Medicaid estate recovery program.

Some highlights of this mandate include the following:

States required to recover any costs for medical help that consists of:

- Nursing home or any other long-term institutional services;

- Any home-and community-based services;

- Hospital and prescription drug services given while the person was getting nursing facility or home-and community-based services; and

- At the state's discretion, any other things that are covered by the Medicaid State Plan.

*****

At the very least, the states are required to recover from any assets that go through the probate process (that is overseen by state law). At the most, they are allowed to recover any assets of the Medicaid recipient who has passed away.

*****

WHOSE ESTATES ARE SUBJECT TO RECOVERY?

Again, that's great and all, but if that's true, then whose estates are subject to recovery?

Another logical question, and a good one.

Any recoveries can only be made from those estates of deceased recipients who were at least 55 or older when they got their Medicaid benefits, or those who, no matter their age, were institutionalized on a permanent basis. Although, states can exempt any recipients if the only benefit they receive is payment of Medicare cost sharing (otherwise known as Medicare Part B premiums).

If a state has chosen to put TEFRA liens on a recipient's home, it has to also recover from the estate of said recipient. The states are allowed to put liens on the property of Medicaid recipients, regardless of age, but only if they are permanently housed in a nursing home or some other kind of medical institution, and if they are expected to pay a portion of the cost of their care in the institution itself.

WHAT EXACTLY IS A MEDICAID RECOVERABLE ESTATE?

OBRA 93, which we mentioned above—the act which mandated the states had to create a Medicaid program—allows those same states to recover, at the very least, any and all property and/or assets that go from a deceased person to his or her heirs under the probate laws set out by the state, like we said before. We got that part.

Probate law, however, is that which presides over both property that is conveyed by the will and property of those who die intestate—that is, without a will. The state's ability to then recover from those probate estates depends on Medicaid's standing regarding their other claimants. The order in which debts are paid is established under the state law. Things such as mortgages, unpaid tax or public utility bills, child support arrears, burial costs, or any other debts can be paid before paying the Medicaid lien. Doing so will result in the reduction of the amount they actually recover. The standing the state has can also be determined by their local priorities. As an example, some state laws protect a family's home in an estate from either some or all claims it may have against it, including those from Medicaid.

A state also has the option to use the narrower definition of "estate"—the Federal definition—and thereby limit those Medicaid estate recoveries to just those assets that go through the probate process. Conversely, they could also choose to define an estate in a broader context, which would then allow them to recover from either some or all property that completely bypasses the probate process.

Such property includes:

- Assets that pass directly to a survivor, heir or assignee through joint tenancy

- Rights of survivorship

- Life estates

- Living trusts

- Annuity remainder payments

- Life insurance payouts

*****

As it is with probate estates, many of those things we listed above operate under some other laws that define both rights and responsibilities in disposition of bank accounts or any other liquid investments, real estate ownership, life insurance policies and more. However, the laws they operate by are most often unrelated to those set out by Medicaid.

Because of this, executing Medicaid laws against those things with a background of non-Medicaid law brings with it the possibility of a lack of legal clarity, potentially competing claims to property of deceased Medicaid recipients, as well as inconsistent outcomes. Even with both legal and practical obstacles when it comes to fully putting an estate recovery program into place—and that program uses the broader definition of estate—it is rather easy to see that the states could potentially increase recoveries by a good amount simply by collecting from those assets that people would otherwise be able to keep safe from the recovery process (that is, they could shift them out of a future probate estate and into a form outside of the reach of Medicaid).

A home is also thought of as part of the recoverable estate, unless it has been protected for use by the spouse or any other close relatives, or is otherwise conveyed outside of the state's definition of an estate (like through a life estate, for example).

HOW MUCH IS SUBJECT TO RECOVERY?

At the very least, the states have to recover any amounts Medicaid spent on long-term care and any related drug and/or hospital benefits. This includes Medicaid payments for any Medicare cost sharing related to those services. Although, they also have the ability to recover costs on *all* Medicaid services they've paid on behalf of the recipient, and a great many states often recover spending for more than that minimum of long-term care and any other related expenses.

States can also choose to waive estate recovery when it has the possibility of not being cost-effective, as the state defines it and as is made public through the state's official Medicaid plan. How the states see the Federal guidance when it comes to this often varies from state to state. Some of them might choose to waive recoveries on smaller estates, or may choose on a case-by-case basis. For example, they could waive recovery when not doing so would be costly because ownership of assets is either complicated or ambiguous in a legal sense, or if the asset is difficult to reach for some other reason altogether.

Any recoveries are not allowed to go beyond the total amount that Medicaid spent on behalf of the recipients at or after the age of 55.

Also, they cannot go beyond the amount that remains in the estate after claims from other creditors against the estate have been settled in that order of debt payment set down by state law, which we talked about earlier.

Those family members or heirs left behind by the recipient cannot be asked to use their own funds in order to repay Medicaid. The only exception to this rule is the possibility that the estate includes the recipient's home. When home equity is brought into the equation, it is then subject to estate recovery by Medicaid. The survivors have the option to sell the home and use any proceeds to pay back Medicaid or pay the claim out of their own personal funds if they want to keep the home in the family.

PROHIBITIONS ON MEDICAID ESTATE RECOVERIES

It might seem like Medicaid has the ability to just steamroll over people and do whatever they want. This, however, is not the case. There are, in fact, some things that Medicaid is prohibited from doing when it comes to estate recoveries.

In those instances where the needs of certain relatives for any assets in the estate have been deemed necessary by Federal law, those trump any claim that Medicaid might have.

Estate recoveries are prohibited:

- During the lifetime of any surviving spouse (no matter where he or she lives).

- When there is a surviving child under age 21, or who is blind or permanently disabled (as defined by the SSI/Medicaid definition of the word), no matter where he or she lives.

*****

Federal guidelines give the implication that states are allowed to begin the recovery process when the surviving spouse passes away, or the child loses his or her protected status, or when a relative who is protected moves out of the house. Although, there are a few states who waive their future right to recovery, still others who defer it, and others who use a variety of approaches depending on the specifics of each individual case.

Federal policies will concede to the states with regard to how they track or monitor any assets that go to protected relatives in those cases where the state keeps its rights to any future recoveries from those survivors of Medicaid recipients. This brings with it some logistical issues however, as it can be difficult to keep track of such things for long periods of time. Not to mention the fact that trying to figure out which of the survivor's assets originally belonged to the recipient brings with it various practical problems too. What's more—some states may wish to waive future recoveries in an effort to avoid the task of collecting from surviving relatives long after the death of their loved one or even years later if and when they decide to move to another home altogether. It isn't known, though, how much potential money Medicaid loses when states opt to do this.

PROCEDURAL RULES

These are put into place so that so that people can be informed about Medicaid program requirements prior to their completion of the application process. States are recommended to tell any applicants about Medicaid estate recovery while they wait to receive their eligibility determination. States can go about estate recovery in a variety of ways, and this depends on their own personal Medicaid program and each state's laws. Although, federal law states that they must mix into their own estate recovery program the following protections for Medicaid recipients.

Let's take a look:

Recipient protections in Medicaid estate recovery:

- The State should let Medicaid recipients know about the estate recovery program at the beginning of the application process to determine eligibility, as well as during the yearly re-determination process.

- The State has to let any affected survivors know of the beginning of the estate recovery process and allow them the chance to claim an exemption because of hardship.

- The State must put into place both procedures and criteria to allow the waiving of recovery if not doing so would cause undue hardship.

*****

It is, however, up to each individual state to create information and put it out there in an effort to bring about a public understanding of the rationale behind Medicaid estate recovery and why it is needed, and they must also inform them of the rights of both the State and the recipient too. Because of this, there is often a lot of variety in the level of resources that each state allows for this process. The state's Medicaid agency has to figure out how to keep it understandable first and foremost, while also covering every necessary point, and also how to accommodate for the variety in each individual's own circumstances.

Decisions must also be reached when it comes to the level of detail that beneficiaries and their loved ones can absorb, along with figuring out when the best time is to give information about estate recovery—a time that may come about long after the application process has come and gone. And even when the state gives all-inclusive information with regard to the estate recovery process at the best time possible, it can still be too much for people—what with all the complexity driving the decisions that they have to make throughout the application process, which can take place in a short, but also emotionally volatile time.

Any efforts by the state to let people know about the estate recovery program are sometimes targets for great amounts of criticism. Of course, states shy away from bad publicity and the kind of litigation that comes from having procedural safeguards that aren't good enough, and they're working to create more correct and thorough information that they can then present to people in a more timely manner as well.

HARDSHIP WAIVERS

It is required for the states to waive any estate recoveries when continuing with the process would end in undue hardship. However, they are allowed a good amount of discretion when it comes to their definition of the word and the impact it would have on their actions with regard to the estate recovery process. As with most things related to the government, there are federal guidelines that have been set which propose two very specific types of property as exceptions for the hardship. They are: those homes of modest value and income-producing property—like farms or family businesses, for example—that are necessary in providing support for those surviving family members.

According to Federal guidelines that have recently been amended, modest homesteads are defined by how they relate to the average value of the homes located in the same county. Nothing is mentioned regarding any limits on value of any income-producing property.

A few of the states surpass these Federal guidelines for waiving or deferring recovery, however. They could potentially negotiate to receive only partial recovery, depending on other definitions of hardship factors given by the State—for example, very low income for any survivors.

Any information on how states go about administering hardship waivers hasn't been published.

Honestly, the topic of estate recovery could be its own book, and we have more things to get through. So, let's finish up this chapter by looking at some pros and cons of estate recovery.

*****

PROS AND CONS OF ESTATE RECOVERY

Those who support a more extensive and aggressive Medicaid when it comes to estate recovery will say that Medicaid is a program for the poor, yes, but one that is chronically needing for money, and that estate recovery programs help to ease some of that burden of paying for long-term care from taxpayers to the estates of those who have received Medicaid. The states are then able to spend their portion of any recovered funds in order to keep or broaden their Medicaid coverage of those services for needy populations, though it isn't something they are required to do.

Those who oppose estate recoveries by Medicaid will stand by their beliefs in its unfairness in the way it affects generally those who have modest means already, while simultaneously sparing the ones who can better get access to advice on techniques for estate planning that work to shelter their assets. Moreover, it also goes against those widely-held cultural values regarding sanctity of intergenerational legacies. Still, others will say that even the threat of estate recovery makes people decline services funded via Medicaid even when they need them, or that it discourages those adult children from trying to get Medicaid for a sick parent, whose health or functioning abilities could potentially worsen as a result. This otherwise avoidable decline could lead to some higher medical costs later.

*****

As you can no doubt tell, this is a very complex subject—as is any portion of Medicaid, or even Medicaid in general. There are a lot of intricate parts and rules and regulations that can be more than a little confusing to the average person or family trying to figure things out. With that in mind, it's certainly recommended to seek the advice of an elder care lawyer—someone who deals in the realm of not only the law and how it affects elders, but also those issues and problems that affect the elder and their families. Knowing that you have the advice and support of an experienced, capable professional can help to bring about peace of mind in what would otherwise be a very difficult and trying time—not only physically, but emotionally as well.

CHAPTER 7

MEDICAID AND COGNITIVE IMPAIRMENTS

For some reason, children often can't wait to grow up, perhaps because they see adults as having so much less in the way of restrictions and so much more in the way of freedom. However, time marches on for each and every one—children and adults alike.

Of course, there are a lot of good things about getting older, such as getting a driver's license, going to college, the freedom to be on your own, and more. Likewise, there are also bad things about getting older too. Eventually, someone may find him or herself unable to move as swiftly or easily as they used to, or they may be unable to remember things they once would have been unable to forget.

The point is that, with as many good things as there are about getting older, it isn't always what it's cracked up to be sometimes. In particular, the elderly face more in the way of health and cognitive issues, and that's going to be our focus for the majority of this chapter. Our goal with this chapter is just to give you a better understanding of cognitive impairments overall; we will cover cognitive issues more in depth in the future.

What we *will* focus on in this chapter is dementia and Alzheimer's. But before we dive into them a little more, perhaps it would be good to say exactly what it is we mean when we talk about cognitive impairment.

So, let's do that now.

WHAT IS COGNITIVE IMPAIRMENT?

In the most general sense, cognitive impairment is simply when someone has trouble with remembering, learning new things, concentrating, or making decisions that can affect their day-to-day lives. It can also range anywhere from mild impairment to more severe. Those suffering from mild impairment could start to notice some changes in their cognitive functions, but still complete their daily activities.

The most severe levels of impairment may cause sufferers to completely lose their ability to understand the meaning or importance of a particular something as well as the ability to talk or write. Understandably, this would mean that the person has lost the ability to live on their own.

Now that we've defined exactly what cognitive impairment is, let's find out more about it.

*****

Sadly, over 16 million people in the United States alone are dealing and living with cognitive impairment in their daily lives. Even so, what this means for states overall isn't well understood. Back in 2009, there were five states that addressed this inadequacy by taking note of the way that cognitive impairment had impacted their residents. Having such knowledge is crucial to creating and keeping more effective policies and programs to be able to meet the needs of those living with cognitive impairment(s) in your own state.

As we said, getting older is the number one risk factor in developing cognitive impairment. Especially with regard to the Baby Boomers— most of whom are over the age of 65, the amount of people dealing with cognitive impairment and its effects on daily life is expected to increase substantially. In fact, there are an estimated 5.1 million people in the U.S. alone who are 65 or older that may potentially suffer from Alzheimer's disease, which is the most well-known and common form of cognitive impairment. By the year 2050, that number could be as high as 13.2 million people.

Also, as with other health issues, dealing with cognitive impairment is not cheap. In fact, those sufferers often report over three times as many hospital stays as those people who are hospitalized for a different reason. Alzheimer's disease and other related dementias are thought to be the third most expensive disease to treat in the country. Back in 2010, the states' average Medicaid expenditure for those suffering from Alzheimer's was estimated to be a whopping $647 million—and this didn't even take home- and community-based care or any prescription drug costs into account.

The looming growth in the number of those who are living with cognitive impairment on a daily basis will not only place greater strain on those people caring for them, but also on the systems of care that have been established to help them. In fact, there are now over 10 million family members giving unpaid care to someone with a cognitive impairment issue, such as a problem with memory or a disease like Alzheimer's or another form of dementia. Back in 2009, that number was estimated to be 12.5 billion hours of unpaid care with a value of $144 billion! Much more in the way of in-home or institutionalized care as well unpaid help by both family and friends will be necessary in the future as the amount of people with Alzheimer's disease or other forms of cognitive impairment continue to grow.

The burden on our economy and the ever-growing need and demand for quality care due to cognitive impairment present quite a challenge to the states in particular and the nation in general. That is, unless certain steps are taken to help ease that burden.

Let's see some ways they can do that:

- State health departments can get more state data to better understand the impact, burden, and needs of those people living with cognitive impairment in their daily lives.

- The states should think about coming up with a more comprehensive plan of action in order to better respond to and meet the needs of those with cognitive impairment, as well as getting different agencies, and both public and private organizations involved too.

- More complex support systems should be built upon for those individuals with cognitive impairment issues as well as their families and caregivers.

- More training is necessary for health professionals to better discover cognitive impairment issues in their earlier stages and provide assistance to those with multiple conditions to manage their care.

*****

By not meeting these needs now, it will mean very serious consequences for those millions of Americans who are affected by cognitive impairment, and not only them, but the state agencies that give both care and services to that particular population.

Now, let's see some key facts about cognitive impairment.

*****

KEY FACTS ABOUT COGNITIVE IMPAIRMENT

Contrary to what we may think or believe, cognitive impairment issues do not stem from any particular disease or condition. Also, it isn't limited simply to a particular age group. Things such as Alzheimer's or other forms of dementia, as well as other conditions like strokes, traumatic brain injuries, and developmental disabilities can contribute to the development of cognitive impairment too.

Below, you'll see some of the most common signs of cognitive impairment. Things like:

- Memory loss

- Frequently repeating the same question or story again and again.

- Being unable to recognize familiar faces or places.

- Having trouble with judgement (i.e. knowing what to do in an emergency situation).

- Changes in mood or behavior

- Vision problems

- Trouble planning and carrying out tasks, like following a recipe or keeping track of any monthly bills.

*****

While age is most definitely a risk factor for suffering cognitive impairment, others can include family history, education level, brain injury, exposure to pesticides or toxins, physical inactivity, and any chronic conditions such as Parkinson's disease, heart disease and stroke, as well as diabetes.

It should be known, though, that people can work to reduce their risk of cognitive impairment by keeping both physically active and keeping their cholesterol and blood sugar levels at a good place. Also, there is currently no cure for cognitive impairment issues caused by things like Alzheimer's or other related dementias. That said, there are some causes of cognitive impairment that are related to health issues that can be treated, such as medication side effects, vitamin B12 deficiency, and depression. This is why it is so necessary to find those people who are exhibiting signs of cognitive impairment to see that they get evaluated by a health care professional and then get the kind of care or treatment they need.

Now, let's look at why cognitive impairment is an important issue.

THE IMPORTANCE OF COGNITIVE IMPAIRMENT

The simple truth is that Americans are afraid of losing their cognitive functions. Truth be told, it isn't just Americans, but *everyone* who dreads this. No one wants to think they might wake up one day and not recognize themselves or their loved ones, or not know where they are. In fact, people are twice as fearful of losing mental capacity as they are having lesser physical ability and it should be said that 60% of adults are either somewhat or very concerned about dealing with potential memory loss.

Those who are affected by cognitive impairment—like adults with Alzheimer's disease, veterans with traumatic brain injuries, and families of those living with cognitive impairment—are representative of a good portion of your population. By taking the right steps to address the issue, it will result in a more positive impact—not only on your community, but your state as a whole.

So, you may be asking what exactly Medicaid's role in all this is.

Let's find out together.

*****

MEDICAID'S ROLE FOR PEOPLE WITH DEMENTIA

Nearly one-half (46%) of those in nursing facilities, and around one in five (21%) elders in the community has either probable or possible dementia. It is a disease that is characterized by chronic and progressive decline in memory and cognitive functions, like communication and judgment. Those sufferers of dementia most often have complicated medical and behavioral health needs, and a great number of them are reliant on family caregivers to help with self-care or other daily activities. As the dementia progresses, it may be necessary to look into getting paid care. In that regard, most people with dementia are Medicare recipients, but the high costs out-of-pocket and a lack of any long-term services and supports (LTSS) coverage may result in those with low income, who also have disabilities resulting from dementia needing Medicaid to help fill in any gaps in coverage.

Speaking of Medicaid, it plays an important role in giving long-term services and supports to those who need it, and is focused more and more on efforts to assist seniors and those with disabilities to stay in the community rather than having to live in an institution.

With the expected growth of the population of elderly over the next few decades and barring any type of medical breakthroughs, it is quite likely that more and more Americans will suffer from dementia, and this also has some implications for Medicaid coverage, delivery system design, financing and quality monitoring as well.

As we said, we'll be taking a look at Medicaid's role for those suffering from dementia in our community, and we'll also pay special attention to common eligibility pathways, characteristics of beneficiaries, any services covered, health care spending and utilization, and key issues with policy.

So, let's get started.

HOW DO PEOPLE WITH DEMENTIA QUALIFY FOR MEDICAID?

Almost a quarter (24%) of adults with dementia living in the

community has Medicaid coverage throughout a year. Almost all adults with dementia (that is, 95%) get benefits from Medicare, and there might be some who also qualify for Medicaid through an age (65+) or disability-related pathway if they also have low income and limited assets. The Medicaid financial eligibility criteria vary from state to state and is also subject to certain federal minimum requirements.

In many states, those who qualify for Supplemental Security Income (or SSI) benefits are automatically eligible to receive Medicaid. In order to be eligible for SSI, however, beneficiaries have to how low incomes (approx. 74% of poverty level), while also having limited assets and being unable to work. The states are also able to give Medicaid coverage to seniors and those people with disabilities who have an income up to 100% of the federal poverty level if they so choose.

What's more—they may also opt to give Medicaid coverage to those who have spent down any excess income or assets in order to meet the threshold for financial eligibility.

*****

People with dementia could also qualify for Medicaid through pathways targeted to those with LTSS needs. A few states extend eligibility for Medicaid to those people who need a certain level of care but have incomes that go above the limits for other pathways. On top of income and asset requirements, these pathways often require people to meet certain functional eligibility criteria—like needing an institutional level of care that is determined by their need for help with a certain amount of activities of daily living, like bathing or eating and/or instrumental activities of daily living like cooking or managing their medications).

These criteria may vary from state to state and eligibility pathways. However, functional eligibility criteria might not always take into account just how much need someone with dementia has. As an example, some functional needs assessments might only account for a need of hands-on help and may not realize there's also a need for verbal or written cues or monitoring in order to complete daily activities—which those with dementia could potentially come up against.

Because of this, not everyone with dementia is eligible to receive Medicaid benefits; instead, that eligibility is dependent on the number of functional needs they have as well as the type of need and the extent of the need.

*****

Not all low-income persons with dementia qualify for or are enrolled in a Medicaid program. A lot of people with dementia often have low incomes but are still not covered by Medicaid. They could be ineligible because they do not meet financial eligibility requirements, or they may not meet the functional criteria for eligibility either. As time goes on, they could use up their resources or income in order to meet care needs, or their functioning may deteriorate to the point that they will not meet eligibility requirements. Alternatively, those who suffer from dementia who also have low incomes might be eligible but be unaware that they *do* qualify for Medicaid benefits, or they could have a hard time with the application process.

Such individuals could attempt to rely on unpaid care from friends or family or pay for their care out-of-pocket, which could potentially be unsustainable over time as they lose more and more of their ability to function properly.

*****

WHO IS THE POPULATION WITH DEMENTIA THAT IS COVERED BY MEDICAID?

Medicaid beneficiaries with dementia will often differ from those who are not covered by Medicaid by gender, race and income. Those Medicaid beneficiaries with dementia are much likelier to be female and are more diverse racially than the portion of population with dementia who doesn't have Medicaid.

Perhaps unsurprisingly, given what we know about Medicaid's criteria for financial eligibility, those beneficiaries with dementia are more likely to have little income than those who aren't covered by Medicaid. As a consequence of this, those beneficiaries with dementia have precious little in the way of financial resources to help pay for their care out-of-pocket. What's more—since nearly half (45%) of those beneficiaries with dementia live alone, it is possible they don't have access to any regular unpaid caregiving from a family member or friend.

*****

Medicaid beneficiaries with dementia are much more likely to report being in fair or poor health as compared to those without Medicaid. Because of their status of poorer health, Medicaid beneficiaries might require more intensive care and/or a broader range of services to help manage their greater health needs. Almost all Medicaid beneficiaries who have dementia (90%) generally have multiple chronic health issues, which might indicate they could benefit from some type of care coordination services and /or some efforts with which to better assimilate medical, behavioral health, and long-term services and supports.

*****

WHAT SERVICES DOES MEDICAID COVER FOR PEOPLE WITH DEMENTIA?

Though a great number of Medicaid beneficiaries are also eligible for Medicare, it should be said that Medicare does not cover all services they might need—especially LTSS. Medicare is, however, the first payer for those beneficiaries who are dually eligible. Medicaid is used just to give wraparound services and to fill in any gaps in coverage.

States that are participating in Medicaid are often required to cover certain services and might allow for other services at state option. Beneficiaries get services based on their medical necessity. Mandatory Medicaid services that could be relevant to those with dementia include both inpatient and outpatient hospital services; lab and x-ray; nursing facility services; home health aide services; including durable medical equipment; physician services; and non-emergency medical transportation.

Optional Medicaid services that could be relevant to people with dementia include prescription drugs; physical therapy and any related services; including speech-language and occupational therapy; private duty nursing; personal care services; hospice case management; adult day health care programs; and respite services. Also, the Affordable Care Act (ACA) allows for a new option as well—Community First Choice, which gives attendant care services and supports with enhanced federal matching funds. In September 2015, five states offered these services (CA, MD, MT, OR, TX).

*****

Some states have taken advantage of the ACA's Medicaid health home option in order to target services to those with dementia. It also gives time-limited enhanced federal funding for the states to give health home services, like case management and care coordination and health promotion, as well as transition services from inpatient to other types of settings, individual and family support, referrals to community and social support services, as well as the use of health information technology in order to link services for those beneficiaries with chronic conditions. Some states, like Alabama, Michigan, New York, and Washington, include dementia among the qualifying conditions for enrollment in their own health home programs, and others offer health home services to those with delusional or chronic cognitive conditions.

*****

Those Medicaid beneficiaries with dementia could also qualify for home and community-based services (HCBS) waivers, some of which could include services that are targeted to those with dementia. As an example, Massachusetts offers a waiver that gives dementia coaching services, while also aiming to divert those frail, elderly beneficiaries from having to go to nursing facilities by giving them services to support them from within in the community.

Virginia also has a waiver aimed at those with dementia, but is limited to assisted living facility services. And unlike the state plan services Medicaid offers, the states are able to place enrollment caps on waiver services, which could possibly result in being placed on a waiting list. HCBS are not always medical in nature and they aim to help those people who have LTSS needs, like those with dementia, reside in their own communities versus having to go to an institution.

*****

WHAT IS UTILIZATION AND SPENDING LIKE FOR MEDICAID BENEFICIARIES WITH DEMENTIA?

Medicaid often has an important role to play in covering any cost of home-based care for those adults with dementia. For services that are covered by Medicare and others, adults who have dementia—both who do and do not have Medicaid—they have quite similar utilization and spending patterns. As an example, there were no real differences between the two groups when it came to the likelihood that they would have a usual source of care, number of office or inpatient visits, and the number of prescriptions.

Likewise, the average per capita total spending and Medicare/other payer spending for the groups was not all that different either. Although, those adults with dementia who *do* have Medicaid are much more likely than those without it to make use of home-based health services. What's more—Medicaid pays an average of $10,805 annually for each adult with dementia, first and foremost for those home-based services.

Since Medicare and many other payers often have incredibly limited coverage of home-based services, those adults with low-incomes who also have dementia aren't likely to be able to afford these kinds of services without getting help from Medicaid.

The effort to get better medical care and LTSS for those with dementia is quite likely to stay a major issue in the arena of public health, as well as being the focus of continuing medical research in the decades to come as policymakers, families, and various other stakeholders consider more cost-effective ways to be able to meet the many needs of this increasingly vulnerable and growing population. Medicaid beneficiaries who have dementia have fewer resources financially to be able to contribute to the cost of care and are much more likely to use home-based health services than those who don't have Medicaid. People suffering from dementia are likely to need paid care as their ability to function properly decreases, and in the absence of other useable public or private financing options, Medicaid will go onto continue being the primary payer in the nation for LTSS.

There are a number of policy issues that will inform the ongoing efforts to better outcomes for health for those Medicaid beneficiaries with dementia in a way that includes them, but that also provides them with a sense of independence and dignity. As an example, those with cognitive impairments—like difficulty communicating, understanding, or retaining new information—could face challenges when it comes to the complexities of the application process for Medicaid benefits. Specialized outreach, education and counseling services might help to ease the process for those with dementia. The states could also see whether their functional needs assessment tools really take note of the full severity, scope and duration of needs that are experienced by those suffering from dementia because of a variety of cognitive impairments.

Also, new efforts in delivering Medicaid services could be targeted toward those with dementia who live in the community. The states now have a wealth of options available to them that they can use to give Medicaid HCBS to better meet the needs of those beneficiaries with dementia. Their efforts to try and integrate medical, long-term, and behavioral health services and supports could be greatly productive, seeing as many beneficiaries with dementia also are suffering from other types of chronic conditions. Furthermore, as the states create programs, those efforts could potentially include the development of dementia-specific measures in order to better assess quality of care, initiatives to keep an adequate number of direct care workers in order to meet the population's needs, and dementia care training as part of provider credentialing in order to promote the best practices possible.

*****

Now that we've covered Medicaid's role for those suffering from dementia, let's now shift our attention a bit and see what it is that they will and will not cover.

DEMENTIA CARE: WHAT'S COVERED AND WHAT'S NOT

Everyone knows that the need for care is greater as dementia worsens. What's more—a lot of people often find themselves wondering exactly what they can expect in the way of long-term care from Medicaid as the disease progresses further.

Perhaps that's been you, perhaps not.

Either way, it is incredibly helpful to know exactly what you can expect them to cover going forward, so let's see that now.

Dementia Care

The journey through dementia begins with custodial care: that is, any routine personal care that doesn't require attention from any specially-trained medical staff. Intermediate care is the next step, and that is when medical care is needed, but not constant; and the next level is skilled care—where the dementia patient needs constant medical care in order to keep what quality of life they are able to.

So, where's Medicaid in all of this?

For a lot of people, Medicaid gives them that provision financially so that those elderly patients can get the level of quality care that they need. A number of options are available for patients depending on whatever level of care they currently need.

In-Home Care

For a lot of dementia patients, in-home care is the much-preferred style of care, and many people wish to sustain this type of care for as long as possible. In-home care also lets the dementia patients get daily visits in order to help with things like personal care and other tasks, such as preparing food, without having to leave home.

In-home care is usually covered by Medicaid. The single qualification would be that the patient would need to be moved to a nursing home or other type of care facility if in-home care is not given.

Adult Day Care Programs

These programs are designed to give care to those individuals who are unable to stay at home by themselves but have no one to care for them during the day. It is also for those who need care but full-time nursing home care is not yet required.

At these types of programs, people with dementia are watched over and cared, and they're able to interact with other adults as well—which can work to keep their minds sharp and functioning for longer than they would be otherwise.

Adult day care programs may be paid for by Medicaid.

Continuing Care Retirement Communities

Continuing care retirement communities (CRCCs) are made to give a tiered approach when it comes to care. For those people who have the ability to live at least somewhat independently, they are afforded that independence. When their condition deteriorates, they are then moved into higher-care levels within the facility.

Normally, Medicaid **does not** pay for these services while the person is completely independent, and oftentimes, people who want to live in a continuing care retirement community have to move in while they still have the ability to live independently in order to secure themselves a place when they are eventually in need of those higher levels of care. As the care needs progress, however, Medicaid may cover assisted living or skilled nursing home care.

Another benefit of this option is that the spouse of the dementia patient can join him or her in the continuing care retirement community.

Adult Family Homes

For the dementia patient, adult family homes can be a great option in receiving continuing care.

In a great many cases, these homes will normally have about six adult patients who are able to interact with each other and with the staff too. They live in a residential home, so the patients are much more comfortable than they might otherwise be in a nursing home-style setting. In adult family homes, occasional medical care is sometimes available if needed.

These services **may or may not be** covered by Medicaid depending on their licensing.

Nursing Home Facilities

When a dementia patient's health gets to the point where they are unable to live alone at all and they require a high level of medical care, a nursing home is most generally their best option.

Nursing homes are designed to get patients the care they so desperately need while keeping up their quality of life for as long as is possible to do so, and Medicaid **will** cover nursing home care for dementia patients.

Memory Care Units

These are specialized facilities that are uniquely designed around the needs of those with dementia and Alzheimer's disease. Within these facilities, patients have the ability to participate in structured activities, and have the ability to be social, get physical therapy and other medical services when they need them, and get their meals brought to them or offered in a dining room.

Patients in memory care units have the option of either private or semi-private rooms, and Medicaid does offer plans that will help to cover the cost of memory care units.

It can be difficult taking care of an elderly loved one anyway, but the financial cost of caring for one who has dementia can be even more so. A lot of people often have trouble finding the right type of care for their loved one, not to mention having to figure out how to pay for it.

That can simply be overwhelming.

We can breathe a sigh of relief though knowing that there are programs like Medicaid that can help families give their loved ones the care they need without breaking the bank. Doing your research and then taking time to consider each available option in any given area will help you to ultimately make the right decision for your loved one's specific needs.

*****

We've reached the end of yet another chapter and are slowly making our way to the end. We still have a little while to go yet before we get to that point, however. While a majority of the book has been focused specifically on Medicaid, there are some other programs—some New Jersey-specific—that we'll take a look at in the next chapter.

See you there.

CHAPTER 8

OTHER PROGRAMS

Welcome back again!

While the book as a whole is and has been about Medicaid overall, there are a few other programs we'd like to talk a little bit about as well. They are, in fact, related to Medicaid, though. So, don't think we got lazy and decided to get sidetracked or anything.

Certainly not.

Instead, we want you to know about as much as you can so that you know what options are available to you when the time comes and you find yourself in need of them. With that in mind, let's take a look at a few of them right now. Our goal for this chapter is to cover a couple of programs and tell you more about ADLs as well—that is, activities of daily living.

Only a little bit more to go until we're finished, so let's get started by talking about PACE.

*****

PROGRAM OF ALL-INCLUSIVE CARE FOR THE ELDERLY (PACE)

As you can see, when we're talking about PACE in this context, we're not talking about running; instead, we're referring to the Program of All-Inclusive Care for the Elderly, otherwise known as PACE. But what exactly *is* PACE and why is it important?

Let's find out together.

PACE is a state-of-the-art program by Medicaid that gives those feeble individuals 55 and older all-inclusive medical and social services that are both coordinated and provided by a group of professionals specializing in different areas of care. This care is given in a center within the community as well as the individual's own homes with the goal of helping the participants in the program to either delay or avoid long-term nursing home care altogether.

Each participant in the program gets specialized care that is geared toward meeting their specific needs given to them by that group of care professionals working at the center. The team will hold regular meetings with participants as well as his or her representative with the goal of figuring out that person's particular needs. The participant's care plan normally includes some home care services provided by that team along with several visits per week to the PACE center itself—which is the hub for all medical care, rehabilitation, social services and dining too.

The PACE program gives participants regular access to both doctors and other primary care professionals who know them and specialize in caring for older individuals. Participants in the PACE program often have better health status and better quality of life, along with lower mortality rates, an increased choice in how they spend their time, and much greater confidence when it comes to dealing with problems in life, according to a recent study.

The financing model for the PACE program combines payments from both Medicaid and Medicare or private pay sources into one flat-rate in order to give people the whole range of health care and services—including paying for hospital care as a response to a person's own unique needs. It also makes use of transportation systems so participants are able to live as independently within the community as they possibly can, while also still having quick access to the supportive services, medical specialists, therapies and other medical care they might need.

These programs will coordinate and provide all preventive, primary, acute and long-term care services older people need so that they may continue to live in the community. PACE is indeed quite an innovative model that allows those people who are at least 55 or older—who are also state-certified to need nursing home care—to be able to live as independently as they possibly can for as long as they can. Through the PACE program, the fragmented health care financing and delivery system of today combines in order to better meet the unique needs of every person in a way that also makes sense to the elderly, their caregivers, health care providers, and policy makers.

WHO IS ELIGIBLE TO PARTICIPATE IN PACE?

In order to participate in PACE, a person must be at least 55 years of age or older. They must also be in need of a nursing home level of care but still be able to live safely in the community at the time they enroll to receive PACE services, as well as live within the service area of a PACE organization. Participants in the PACE program can unenroll at any time, for any reason, and anyone who unenrolls who has Medicare or Medicaid will be helped in returning to the health coverage they had before.

What Services Does PACE Provide?

The PACE program affords every participant all the services that are covered by Medicare and Medicaid, without any of the limitations that are normally imposed by those programs. It also gives them any other services that the person's care team has deemed necessary if it would let the program participants stay in the community.

Some of the services provided by PACE include but are not limited to the following:

- **Primary care (including doctor, dental and nursing services),**

- **Prescription drugs,**

- **Adult day health care,**

- **Home and personal care services,**

- **Nutrition services, and**

- **Hospital and nursing home care if and when needed**

The program also provides any transportation both to and from the center and any and all off-site medical appointments if needed.

What You Pay Depends on Your Financial Situation

This capitated arrangement for funding gives rewards to providers who are flexible and creative when it comes to giving high quality care and affords them the ability to coordinate care across multiple settings and medical disciplines. It also accepts those who choose to pay privately. If you have Medicaid, you're not going to need to pay a monthly premium for the long-term care portion of your PACE benefit.

If, however, you don't qualify for Medicaid but have Medicare, you'll be charged for the following:

- A monthly premium to cover the long-term care portion of your PACE benefits

- A premium for Medicare Part D drugs

When Did PACE come to New Jersey?

There were, in fact, two PACE agencies that began operations in New Jersey in 2009; a third in 2010; a fourth in 2011; and a fifth in 2015. The program is currently offered in 65 markets across the nation and has been in development in New Jersey since all the way back in 2004, the time when the State got a grant from U.S. Centers for Medicare and Medicaid Services (CMS) and technical help from the National PACE Association in order to study bringing the programs to the state. Besides putting money into feasibility studies to figure out the best locations for PACE, the National PACE Association award gave education to state staff, and outreach to communities and any potential providers.

The PACE model itself was developed in San Francisco back in the 1970s as ON LOK, the Chinese-American community's alternative to nursing homes. It was then formally established by CMS as a permanent Medicare Advantage Plan in 1997.

Is PACE Available in My Community?

- Five PACE agencies are currently operating in New Jersey and you have to live in the coverage area but they are looking to add more

- How do I get more information on PACE?

  o Call the New Jersey Division of Aging Services toll-free at 1-800-792-8820, or you can contact the PACE agencies currently in operation:

- LIFE St. Francis: 609-599-5433

- LIFE at Lourdes: 856-675-3675

- Lutheran Senior LIFE: 877-543-3188

- Inspira LIFE: 855-295-5433

- Beacon of LIFE: 732-592-3400

*****

JERSEY ASSISTANCE FOR COMMUNITY CAREGIVING (JACC)

Unlike the PACE program, the Jersey Assistance for Community Caregiving (also known as JACC) is not a Medicaid program and has no relation to it. Its purpose is to serve those who are otherwise ineligible to receive Medicaid, and is paid for solely with state funds. It works to give program participants various in-home services to allow them the opportunity to remain in their community homes when they would otherwise have to move into a nursing home. However, they must also meet both the income and resource requirements necessary to do so.

In giving them a package of supports that have been specially designed for each person, JACC is able to delay or prevent being placed in a nursing home altogether.

Now, let's see some of the services they may provide.

Potential Services

A Plan of Care (POC) is created in collaboration with the patient and his or her Care Manager in response to the results of a clinical assessment. All participants in the JACC program have their own Care Management services. What's more—the Plan of Care notes any other services that should be delivered to the patient.

They can include:

- Respite Care

- Homemaker Services

- Environmental Accessibility Adaptations

106

- Personal Emergency Response Systems (PERS)

- Home-Delivered Meal Service

- Caregiver/Recipient Training

- Special Medical Equipment and Supplies

- Transportation

- Chore Services

- Attendant Care

- Home-Based Supportive Care

*****

Are there limits to JACC services?

In fact, there *are* limits to the services, as cost caps are put on specific services under JACC along with the cost per person per month. JACC services are limited to $600/month or $7,200/year maximum. The entire service package is given based on an assessment of each person's needs, their own personal care plan, and the availability of the services and funding.

Who provides these services?

JACC services can be provided by traditional Waiver service providers, new non-traditional qualified entities, or qualified Participant-Employed Providers. Any and all service providers have to show competence in the service they are providing and must also meet all of the qualification requirements. Individuals that choose the Participant-Employed Provider service option have the opportunity to work directly with their own personal Care Manager to be able to employ their own provider and be in direction of their own care. And speaking of directing their own care, that ability will be confirmed before their participation in being an employer of their own providers.

Qualification Requirements for JACC

In order to qualify for JACC, an individual has to be:

- A resident of New Jersey and at least 60 years of age or older.

- In need of nursing home level of care but wishes to stay at home.

- Not financially eligible for Managed Long-Term Services and Supports or other NJ FamilyCare Programs

- Not participating in the NJ Alzheimer's Adult Day Services Program or Statewide Respite Care Program

- Have resources either at or below $40,000 for one person and $60,000 for a couple.

- A U.S. citizen or qualified alien.

- Have no other means to get the support they need.

- Live in the community and not in an assisted living, nursing home, or residential care facility.

*****

Now that we've covered both of those programs, let's focus our attention on another issue facing the elderly—Activities of Daily Living (ADLs). We'll take a quick look at what they are and how they may affect the eligibility of someone to receive Medicaid benefits.

ACTIVITIES OF DAILY LIVING AND MEDICAID ELIGIBILITY

In your journey of caregiving thus far, you may have come across the initials ADL. They stand for Activities of Daily Living, and those are exactly what they seem like they would be—important activities that most of us do each and every day without a second thought.

For the elderly, however, these activities may become more difficult, if not impossible to do over time. Before we get further into that, though, let's take a bit to recap.

So, in order to qualify for Medicaid, the DCF caseworker is looking to see if the Medicaid applicant meets the eligibility standards that have been put into place.

There are three broader tests they look at:

- **Medicaid Asset Test:** The applicant has to have $2,000 or less in any countable assets (though certain ones are exempt and will not be counted toward Medicaid's resource limits).

- **Medicaid Income Test:** The applicant must make less than $2,205.00 per month in income from any and all sources (such as social security, pension withdrawals, annuity payments, investment income, and wages). It would be good to speak with an elder law attorney to talk about ways to both legally and ethically qualify you or your loved one to receive Medicaid benefits.

- **Medicaid Needs Test:** After both the income and asset standards have been met, there has to also be a medical need to have Medicaid's long-term care services (also referred to as ICP) before being admitted into a nursing home (under the Medicaid ICP program). The Department of Elder Affairs will have a representative conduct a Comprehensive Assessment and Review for Long-Term Care Services—also known as a CARES Assessment or the CARES Program. This program will be looking at the Medicaid applicant's ability to perform the six activities of daily living.

Activities of Daily Living

As we said, there are six standards of Activities of Daily Living (ADLs). They include whether or not the applicant can carry out the following six activities. The first three revolve around functional activities:

1. **Dress Themselves**

2. **Transfer (go from sitting to standing, and vice versa) and maneuver to a chair or to their bed**

The next three refer to those activities that are necessary for both hygiene and sustenance:

3. **Bathe/Shower themselves**

4. **Feed themselves**

5. **Use a toilet themselves**

6. **Continence**

In general, if the applicant is unable to perform two of the six ADLs, they may be considered to be in need of care and, thus, be approved for the program assuming other requirements are met.

*****

So, that's it for this chapter. Coming up, we'll take a look at how things can go wrong with Medicaid. Just a little further to go and we'll be finished!

Stick around!

CHAPTER 9

MYTHS, FACTS, AND MISTAKES

Since we've come so far in this book already, it would be nice to change things up just a bit. To do that, let's kick things off by taking a look at some myths and truths regarding the spenddown requirement. Since it's tied into Medicaid as well, it would do good to make sure we're getting the right information.

MYTHS AND TRUTHS ABOUT THE SPENDDOWN REQUIREMENT

1. Myth: Annuities are not allowed.

Truth: The spouse will be instructed to spend down the excess assets on things like irrevocable funeral contracts, household improvements and nursing home costs. After that amount has been both properly and completely used up, the spouse would then be eligible to receive assistance from Medicaid.

However, there is a way to meet that spend-down requirement without having to continue paying for nursing home costs, and that way is this: the Medicaid annuity.

Federal laws allow for the excess assets (i.e. the "spend-down amount") to be converted into a stream of income and then protected from spend-down by putting those assets into an immediate annuity. As long as that annuity conforms to both federal and state statutes, the amount of funds put into the annuity shouldn't be considered as a countable asset. The transfer of those assets into a qualifying annuity should also not be subjected to any look-back period; the purchase of this kind of annuity is deemed as a transaction for fair market value and not a gift.

A good example of this is a couple that owns a home, vehicle, a few life insurance policies, a modest stock portfolio and the normal checking and savings accounts. The home, all of its contents, and the vehicle are counted as exempt assets when one spouse still lives in the community. For 2017, state and federal laws allow the at-home spouse to keep the greater of $24,180, or one-half of any non-exempt assets, up to a maximum amount of $120,900 (this amount changes yearly with increases in the Federal Consumer Price Index).

The couple above could buy an immediate qualifying annuity and then convert the resource into a stream of income for the benefit of the at-home spouse. This could also be done with an IRA annuity.

You should be aware that a Medicaid annuity has a lot of qualifying parameters. The annuity has to conform precisely or it will be considered a countable asset by the state and then further act to disqualify the institutionalized spouse to receive Medicaid help.

The annuity needs to be "actuarially sound," that is, it has to be written for a term that is no longer than the annuitant's life expectancy as set forth in the Actuarial Life Tables that is published by the Social Security Administration and has to provide for equal payments to the contract owner (no balloon payments).

The annuity also has to be irrevocable and non-assignable. Once it has been purchased, the owner is unable to revoke the contract and request a refund. Neither is he or she able to trade or assign the income stream to someone else for a lump-sum payout or as a gift.

Finally, the annuity has to either (a) name the State of New Jersey as the primary remainder beneficiary for at least the total amount of medical assistance (Medicaid) paid on behalf of the annuitant or spouse; or (b) name the State of New Jersey as the contingent beneficiary after the community spouse or minor or disabled child and the state is named as primary beneficiary if such spouse or a representative of the child disposes of any remainder interest for anything less than fair market value.

Consequently, without regard to which spouse is the actual owner of the annuity, the state has to be named as a remainder beneficiary. With that said, if the annuitant can survive the term of the annuity, he or she will have gotten all of the couple's funds in return, with nothing more to pay the State. These funds can then be used for his or her own continued care.

2. Myth: I have to give away everything I own to get Medicaid.

Truth: There are certain assets that are non-countable or exempt and, thus, are not typically considered when someone applies to receive Medicaid benefits. These include the following: the primary residence with certain equity restrictions; a motor vehicle (sometimes of limited value); personal belongings and household furnishings; funeral trusts; $2,000 and life insurance with a face value of $1,500 or less.

3. Myth: The State will take my house.

Truth: Federal law requires each state to seek reimbursement of medical assistance paid through the Medicaid program. Repayment is sought after the death of the Medicaid recipient through a claim against the decedent's estate.

4. Myth: I have to wait 3 years after giving away to get Medicaid.

Truth: Effective for any and all transfers on or after February 8, 2006, there is now a 5-year lookback period (which we've talked about previously). Certain transfers are exempt from the transfer penalty, including transfers to spouses and any children with disabilities. For all other transfers made within the lookback period, a transfer penalty calculation is applied when an application for Medicaid long-term care benefits is filed. The most significant change in Medicaid law since February 8, 2006, is the start date for the ineligibility period caused by a transfer. For those transfers that pre-date the change in the law, the penalty period started in the month the transfer was made. Now, the penalty period begins only after the Medicaid application is filed and the applicant is determined to otherwise be entitled to receive Medicaid but for the penalty.

5. Myth: I can keep all our marital property and my inherited property when my spouse gets Medicaid.

Truth: When someone who is married applies for Medicaid nursing home benefits, assets in the name of either spouse or in the joint names of both spouses (his, hers or theirs) are considered by Medicaid. As we said above, there are some assets that are exempt. Along with those exempt assets, a spouse that remains at home can keep the Community Spouse Resource Allowance which is one-half of the non-exempt assets, up to a maximum of $120,900 in 2017. In some cases, the allowance for the community spouse can be increased. Inherited property is included in this calculation; however, an inheritance received by the community spouse after a determination of eligibility will not be included.

6. Myth: My spouse or agent under my Power of Attorney has the power to take property out of my name if I ever need Medicaid.

Truth: The best tool for planning for future Medicaid eligibility is a general durable power of attorney for finances that also includes gifting authority. Simply being married does not mean one spouse is able to legally remove the name of an incapacitated spouse from real estate and bank accounts. And unless a power of attorney explicitly authorizes the agent to make gifts of the principal's property, the agent also cannot re-title assets. Specifically, he or she may not make gifts to themselves unless the documents so authorize them to do so.

A lot of powers of attorney do not contain gifting authority or, if they do, the power is inadequate. As an example, many documents have a gifting provision that limits the agent to making transfers of annual exclusion gifts of $14,000 per year per person. Such a figure is too limited for, and irrelevant to, effective Medicaid planning.

7. Myth: I can give away $14,000 per year under Medicaid rules.

Truth: This figure is known as the "annual exclusion amount." This concept is important in planning to minimize estate and gift taxes, but it has no relevance when it comes to planning for Medicaid eligibility.

*****

Now that all of that information is out of the way, let's finish up this chapter by looking at the top ten Medicaid mistakes.

Top Ten Medicaid Mistakes

1. **Believing Medicare or health insurance pays for long-term assisted living or nursing home care.** It doesn't. You have to pay for it unless you plan properly.

2. **Public benefits (Medicaid) is only for the poor.** Back in 1965, this government public benefit program started off this way; although, there is no other government plan available to seniors to avoid long-term care cost impoverishment (a $144,000 yearly cost in many quality nursing homes) other than private long-term care insurance. Because of this, Medicaid pays 65% of the costs of long-term care of middle and upper middle class assisted living and nursing facility residents across the country.

3. **Thinking it's too late to plan.** It is never too late to start planning for long-term care, even after a family member becomes a resident in a nursing home.

4. **Gifting assets directly to children.** It's your money, house, or both. You have to be able to take care of yourself first. You don't want to risk financial security by transferring *everything* to your children. If they have marital, creditor, or addiction issues you aren't aware of, gifting directly to them can be detrimental. Impulsive transfers can cause difficulties with taxes, healthcare and Medicaid eligibility. If you plan properly for things, you will be able to keep them in control perhaps through the use of a specific type of trust.

5. **Ignoring Congress's "safe harbors."** There are certain transfers that are allowed without putting your eligibility for Medicaid benefits at risk. They include the following: transfers to disabled children, a caretaker child, certain siblings or into a trust for a child or another party who is a minor, blind, disabled or under age 65; transfers to a "Special Needs Trust" or pooled disability trust of any accident settlement proceeds or an inheritance that is received after a person is on Medicaid or Supplemental Security Insurance

6. **Failing to use protections for the spouse of a nursing home resident.** These include the total sheltering of a home from a spouse's medical spend down; petitioning from the "at home" community spouse for an increase in the limited Medicaid resource or income allowance, shelter of the at-home spouse's IRA/401k/403b from the other spouse's medical spend down.

7. **Applying for Medicaid too early/too late.** Apply for Medicaid too early and you'll have a longer period of ineligibility. Too late, and you can have needless spend down and a loss of several months of eligibility you would otherwise have.

8. **Not getting expert help.** Filling out a Medicaid application can be very difficult, and dealing with the process is something that a great many people and/or their attorneys deal with only a handful of times in their entire lives. Tens or hundreds of thousands of dollars are at risk here. This is why it is so important to make an appointment with an elder law attorney, who can help guide you through such an overwhelming process. After all, they do it on a daily basis. They're good at what they do, and you deserve the best help you can get when dealing with something so confusing.

9. **Tax and Estate Planning should also include health care planning.** All three concepts are things that are considered by elder lawyers and their partners, and are coordinated to help avoid issues in the future. For example, a yearly gift of $14,000.00 per person is allowed under the IRS gift tax rules—that are widely used when it comes to estate planning. But be warned, that same transfer causes the giver to become ineligible for Medicaid for months. Consulting with an elder law attorney can help you figure everything out, and make the process so much simpler.

CHAPTER 10

SHOULD I HIRE AN ATTORNEY?

If you've made it this far, congratulations!

You've made it to the end of this book. This is the final chapter, and it's going to be a short one. Now, let's take time to answer one final question: should you hire an attorney?

The short answer is simply: yes.

We've covered so much information throughout our time together in this book that it would be too much for any one person to try and wrap their minds around on their own. That's why it is, in fact, so important to seek the help of professionals whose job it is to guide people just like you through situations involving planning for the care of yourself or your elderly loved one. After all, you want to make sure that you get either the kind of care that either they or you deserve.

Trying to go this road alone can lead to not only a lot of confusion, but you also run the risk of overlooking something that would be vital to you otherwise. You want to make sure, especially when trying to decide on Medicaid or, if you already have it, dealing with all that comes with it, that you know exactly what it is you're doing and what you can expect from each and every step in the process.

That's where attorneys like me and my colleagues come in. As I mentioned above, it is our job, and not only that—it is the reason we wake up every day. Because we are motivated, driven by a desire to help people like yourself and your loved ones get the information you need *before* you reach the point of actually needing it. That way, when that time *does* come—no matter if that time is now or later on down the road—you can face it head on, with confidence in yourself and those who are on your team.

There's no doubt that facing the reality of getting older can be scary. But there's something important that we must remember—

It doesn't have to be.

The simple truth of the matter is this: If we live long enough, we get older. It may seem silly when you read that aloud or to yourself, but it's the truth isn't it?

Getting older happens to all of us, so there *is* some comfort to be found in that knowledge too. When we're dealing with getting older and all the issues that come with it, it can seem overwhelming, like a crushing weight, and that's where people like me come in.

We want to help you, to work with you to ease those burdens, and to lift you out from under the crushing weight and confusion of Medicaid, health issues and all of those decisions swirling around. You aren't the only one facing this exact situation in this exact moment.

You certainly shouldn't be made to feel like you are.

RESOURCES

The information contained in this book was provided by the following sources:

""Applying for Medicaid." *State of New Jersey*, http://www.state.nj.us/humanservices/dmahs/clients/medicaid/what_you_need_to_know_medicaid.pdf. Accessed 4 Sept. 2017.

"Applying for Medicaid." *Applying for Medicaid - Long-Term Care Information*, 21 Feb. 2017, http://longtermcare.acl.gov/medicare-medicaid-more/medicaid/applying-for-medicaid.html. Accessed 22 Aug. 2017.

"Avoid Medicaid Mistakes." *Patel Law Offices*, 19 Dec. 2015, http://patellawoffices.com/wills-trusts-and-estate-planning/new-jersey-medicaid/avoid-medicaid-mistakes/. Accessed 4 Sept. 2017.

"Benefits Application." *Tucson*, http://benefitsapplication.com/apply/NJ/Medicaid. Accessed 10 Aug. 2017.

"Cognitive Impairment: A Call for Action, Now!" *Centers for Disease Control*, The Centers for Disease Control, http://www.cdc.gov/aging/pdf/cognitive_impairment/cogimp_poilicy_final.pdf. Accessed 4 Sept. 2017.

"Dementia Care: What's Covered by Medicaid and What's Not." *Alzheimers.net*, 16 Oct. 2015, http://www.alzheimers.net/10-16-15-dementia-care-whats-covered-by-medicaid/. Accessed 26 Aug. 2017.

Eghrari, Mark. "The Medicaid Look Back Period Explained." *Forbes*, Forbes Magazine, 1 Aug. 2014, http://www.forbes.com/sites/markeghrari/2014/08/01/the-medicaid-look-back-period-explained/#6cb7d3f81364. Accessed 8

Aug. 2017.

"Eligibility." *Medicaid.gov*, www.medicaid.gov/medicaid/eligibility. Accessed 8 Aug. 2017.

Garfield, Rachel, et al. "Medicaid's Role for People with Dementia." *The Henry J. Kaiser Family Foundation*, 19 Oct. 2015, http://www.kff.org/medicaid/issue-brief/medicaids-role-for-people-with-dementia/. Accessed 26 Aug. 2017.

"How do I apply for Medicaid?" *Medicare Interactive*, http://www.medicareinteractive.org/get-answers/programs-for-people-with-limited-income/medicaid-and-medicare/how-do-i-apply-for-medicaid. Accessed 11 Aug. 2017.

"How to Qualify for Medicaid | PA, NJ Medicaid Planning." *Medicaid Planning | Medicaid Applications | Medicaid Plus | PA, NJ, NY, MD, DE*, http://www.mymedicaidplus.com/faqs.html. Accessed 16 Aug. 2017.

"Jersey Assistance for Community Caregivers." *County of Warren, NJ - Department of Human Services*, http://www.co.warren.nj.us/humanservices/jacc.html. Accessed 15 Aug. 2017.

"Jersey Assistance for Community Caregiving." *Department of Human Services | Jersey Assistance for Community Caregiving (JACC)*, http://www.nj.gov/humanservices/doas/services/jacc/. Accessed 15 Aug. 2017.

"Jersey Assistance for Community Caregiving (JACC)." *Family and Children's Service*, http://fcsmonmouth.org/what-we-do/community-support-services/jersey-assistance-for-community-caregiving-jacc/. Accessed 15 Aug. 2017.

Kraham, Bonnie. "Bonnie Kraham: The gifting dichotomy: Medicaid vs. IRS rules." *Recordonline.com*, Recordonline.com, 21 Dec. 2016, http://www.recordonline.com/news/20161221/bonnie-kraham-gifting-dichotomy-medicaid-vs-irs-rules. Accessed 10 Aug. 2017.

Marinaro, Lauren. "The Medicaid Fair Hearing Process What You Need To Know." *Medicaid Fair Hearing, How to Appeal | Elder Law Attorneys in NJ*, 1 Dec. 2014, http://www.finkrosner.com/articles/medicaid-fair-hearing-process.html. Accessed 19 Aug. 2017.

Matthews, Joseph L. *How Medicaid Works.* 23 Aug. 2017, http://www.caring.com/articles/how-does-medicaid-work. Accessed 4 Sept. 2017.

"Medicaid Eligibility for the Supports Program." *NJ Division of Developmental Disabilities*, Mar. 2016, http://www.nj.gov/humanservices/ddd/documents/medicaid_eligib ility_for_supports_program.pdf. Accessed 22 Aug. 2017.

"Medicaid Estate Recovery." *ASPE*, 21 Feb. 2017, http://aspe.hhs.gov/basic-report/medicaid-estate-recovery. Accessed 23 Aug. 2017.

Medicaid in New Jersey. http://medicaid-help.org/new-jersey-medicaid-insurance. Accessed 14 Aug. 2017.

Neufeld, Jason. "Activities of Daily Living and Medicaid Eligibility | Blog." *Neufeld, Kleinberg & Pinkiert, PA*, 23 Feb. 2017, http://www.elderneedslaw.com/blog/activities-of-daily-living-and-medicaid-eligibility. Accessed 15 Aug. 2017.

"New Jersey Cost and Coverage." *Medicaid-Help.org*, http://medicaid-help.org/New-Jersey-Cost-and-Coverage. Accessed 14 Aug. 2017.

New York State Office of Temporary and Disability Assistance. "Frequently Asked Questions | Fair Hearings." *New York State Office of Temporary and Disability Assistance*, http://otda.ny.gov/hearings/faq.asp. Accessed 10 Aug. 2017.

"The New jersey Medicaid Program and Estate Recovery -What You Should Know." *The Official Website for The State of New Jersey,* http://www.nj.gov/humanservices/dmahs/clients/The_NJ_Medicaid_Program_and_Estate_Recovery_What_You_Should_Know.pdf. Accessed 4 Sept. 2017.

"The Split Gift Plan (Curing Penalized Gifts)." *Williger Legal Group LLC,* 8 July 2014, http://willigerlegalgroup.wordpress.com/2014/07/08/the-split-gift-plan-curing-penalized-gifts/. Accessed 8 Aug. 2017.

What does Medicare cover (Parts A, B, C, and D)? http://www.medicareinteractive.org/get-answers/introduction-to-medicare/explaining-medicare/what-does-medicare-cover-parts-a-b-c-and-d. Accessed 9 Aug. 2017.

"What is Medicare?" *Medicare Interactive,* http://www.medicareinteractive.org/get-answers/introduction-to-medicare/explaining-medicare/what-is-medicare. Accessed 9 Aug. 2017.

"What is the difference between Medicare and Medicaid?" *Medicare Interactive,* http://www.medicareinteractive.org/get-answers/introduction-to-medicare/explaining-medicare/what-is-the-difference-between-medicare-and-medicaid. Accessed 9 Aug. 2017.

"What is the Medicaid Look-Back Period? What Penalties, Exemptions & Workarounds Exist?" *Medicaid's Look-Back Period Explained: Exceptions & Penalties,* Sept. 2016, http://www.payingforseniorcare.com/medicaid/look-back-period.html. Accessed 17 Aug. 2017.

"Your Peace of Mind is Our Priority." *Medicaid Qualified Income Trust (Miller Trust),* http://www.karplaw.com/page/qualified-income-trust. Accessed 11 Aug. 2017.

Made in the USA
Middletown, DE
08 July 2022